Please return / renew by date shown.
You can renew at: **norlink.norfolk.gov.uk**
or by telephone: **0344 800 8006**
Please have your library card & PIN ready.

NORFOLK LIBRARY
AND INFORMATION SERVICE
NORFOLK ITEM

DEDICATION

*I would like to dedicate this book
to YOU, the reader.*

Thank you

WHAT'S THA PLAYING AT NAH?

Martyn Johnson

PEN & SWORD
TRUE CRIME

First published in Great Britain in 2016 by
Pen & Sword True Crime
an imprint of
Pen & Sword Books Ltd
47 Church Street
Barnsley
South Yorkshire
S70 2AS

ISBN 978 1 47385 812 1

Typeset in Ehrhardt by
Mac Style Ltd, Bridlington, East Yorkshire
Printed and bound in the UK by CPI Group (UK) Ltd,
Croydon, CR0 4YY

Pen & Sword Books Ltd incorporates the imprints of Pen &
Sword Archaeology, Atlas, Aviation, Battleground, Discovery,
Family History, History, Maritime, Military, Naval, Politics,
Railways, Select, Transport, True Crime, and Fiction,
Frontline Books, Leo Cooper, Praetorian Press, Seaforth
Publishing and Wharncliffe.

For a complete list of Pen & Sword titles please contact
PEN & SWORD BOOKS LIMITED
47 Church Street, Barnsley, South Yorkshire, S70 2AS,
England
E-mail: enquiries@pen-and-sword.co.uk
Website: www.pen-and-sword.co.uk

Contents

Foreword

by Chris Mann

I've known Martyn *Fred* Johnson, for over thirty years; and during that time we've laughed and we've cried. We've watched our children through the ages, from birth to raising children of their own. A lifetime has passed, seemingly in a split second. But, what quality!

Over those years Martyn's tales would come thick and fast and with that unforgettable and, so genuine, broad Darfield accent. Martyn has the rare ability of a good storyteller: to make the stories come to life. Over the years, both I and lots of his pals have tried to encourage him to write a book, which he has now done with great success.

Martyn does not suffer fools easily but if you're a pal of his, which I certainly am, then you're a dear and genuine friend for life.

His books include stories from someone who actually took part in the events which he portrays. The highs, the lows of policing in what was, a seemingly friendlier era.

Martyn's *What's Tha Playing at Nah?* paints a vivid picture of life in South Yorkshire, when he was proud to be a 'copper'. Just read, enjoy, and become part of it.

Acknowledgements

If someone had told me six years ago that I would write a book about life as a 'bobby', I'd have laughed at them. I'm more of a reader than a writer and before I wrote my first book, *What's Tha Up To?* the only writing that I'd previously done was police reports and the odd postcard or two.

Luckily, just like my mum Esther, who passed away just short of her hundredth birthday, I've been blessed with a good memory, which, of course, is very handy when writing your memoirs. I also love people and laughter, something that I have often used when trying to get out of a tricky situation or a fight.

Like all 'old bobbies' I have many stories to tell and now here we are on book number four – unbelievable – and all because of you, the reader, who keeps asking for more.

A detective's job by its very nature is often more serious than when you are working a beat – something that I couldn't wait to get back to doing. Anyway you'll read more about that in book 5, which my publishers have already asked me to write.

Writing a book is no easy task and especially so for a 'thicko' like me. Without the help of my fabulous wife, Christine, who has the patience and typing skills to turn my scribblings into something both logical and legible, I would be unable to do it – thanks very much Christine – love you loads.

I must also thank once more my editor and friend Brian Elliott for his continued patience and support; also Matt Jones and the staff at Pen & Sword Books Ltd; and my pal Chris Mann for writing the Foreword.

Since writing this series of books I have received hundreds of wonderful letters and emails, not just from this country, but from around the world, including cruise ships – which amazes me. I am and always will be a 'people person' and for that reason, without listing loads of names, I would like to say thank you to you all – please see the dedication.

Please note that some of the names mentioned in this book have been changed to protect the identity of the person mentioned.

CHAPTER 1

Clubs and Cubs!

What a MESS! But at least he was still alive. Both his eyes were badly swollen and closing up; and you could also see where his broken front teeth had cut through his lips. No wonder there was blood everywhere – pouring from his broken nose and mouth; and running down his face, splattering onto the tiled toilet floor. So much for a quiet night, I thought.

It was a weekday evening and I'd started work at a police station in the grimy industrial east end of Sheffield called Attercliffe. I was on night duty, starting at 11 pm, and had just taken over from my fellow detective John Longbottom who, luckily for him, had had a quiet evening – most unusual for our very busy police division. I needed to take some court papers up to the charge office in relation to a case I was dealing with and John had asked if he could cadge a lift up to town where he had agreed to meet a police informant (or 'snout') in the Cavendish night club on Bank Street, in the middle of Sheffield.

After dropping off the paperwork at the charge office, John and I walked across the road to one of the most popular night clubs in the north of England, where many famous musicians, comedians, singers and pop groups had appeared whilst making their way to the top of the celebrity tree. It also meant that I could have a swift pint, a rarity on nights.

All night clubs have bouncers or doormen, quite rightly looking after their customers and that night was no exception. As we arrived we could see several bouncers wrestling on the floor with two guys who were covered in blood. The doormen had obviously got the situation under control and I recognized two detectives from the City Division standing nearby.

'Everything alright lads?' John asked the detectives.

'Yes,' was the reply, 'we've got em but I'm not sure for what yet. They were trying to run out of the club and, as they were covered in blood, the doormen grabbed them and stopped them leaving realizing that something was wrong.'

The detectives were obviously dealing with some sort of incident or other so John and I entered the club, showed our warrant cards at reception and went to the bar for a pint. John, who was a tight old bugger, was ordering two beers. Wow I thought, that's a first. I'll bet that we'd not been in the club three minutes when 'Big Derek', the head doorman, rushed up to me and said, 'Mr Johnson I think you'd better come to the gents toilets and look at the guy inside.'

'Why Derek, what's up?' I replied, 'I haven't even got a pint yet.'

Derek was very agitated, so I followed him to the gent's toilets and that's when I went in and saw the poor chap already mentioned. I could see that, although unconscious, the bloke was still alive but certainly not kicking!

'Have you sent for an ambulance, Derek?' I asked.

'Yes, it's on its way,' he replied somewhat anxiously.

With that I stepped back out of the toilet cubicle in order to take stock of the situation further. As I looked at the bloke who was sitting on the toilet with his head lolled back and resting on the cistern I knew at once that it had taken at least two chaps to administer this savage beating. One guy at least must have come up behind him, reached over his shoulders and grabbed the big guy's jacket lapels; and then pulled his jacket backwards over his shoulders and down as far as his elbows. It was one of the oldest tricks in the world; and would have totally restricted the movement of his arms, meaning that he would have been unable to defend himself.

There was no blood outside the cubicle and it appeared to me that the man had then been pushed backwards into the cubicle, landing on the seat of the toilet with his jacket and sleeves still wrapped round his elbows. He wouldn't have stood a chance, as the savage beating took place.

Whoever had done the 'job' had then ripped and spread open the man's shirt and he had then slashed him with a knife right across his bare chest, leaving two long and nasty cuts in the shape of a 'kiss' or 'cross'. These cuts stretched from either side of the top of his rib cage and down to his waist on the opposite side of his body. The same thing had also been done to the man's cheeks – a deep cross carved on each one. No wonder there was so much blood. The assailants had then tried to leave the club in a hurry before anyone found the injured man, but being covered in blood themselves and coupled with the fact that they were running out, the bouncers realized that something was amiss; and detained them. Well done lads.

It was a professionally done job alright and it was quite apparent that had they wished to have killed him they could have done just that. By beating and then carving the man up in such a way meant to me, that should he live (and luckily for him he did) then he would bear the scars for the rest of his life to remind him of the fact that he had crossed and upset someone.

The ambulance men and John arrived together at the toilets and John got a shock. As the ambulance lads were putting him on a stretcher John whispered to me, 'Bloody hell Martyn, that's the bloke who I've come to meet!'

By this time Big Derek had fetched one of the city detectives to the scene who then saw for himself the reason why the assailants were covered in blood; and also trying to flee the club. They had found the knife which was used in the attack hidden down the side of one of the assailant's sock and they were then taken into custody and charged with the serious offence. The detectives and John along with the ambulance then left the club leaving me at last to enjoy a quiet pint.

A few months prior to this incident, John had been contacted by the snout about a chap who was making a damned good living swindling jewellers throughout the north. Apparently his MO (method of operation) was to go along to classy shops with his classy bird who flashed plenty of flesh thus bamboozling the jewellers. She would try on lots of expensive rings pretending to be a prospective purchaser and her partner in crime would exchange one or two with cheap fakes; and it was only when they had left the shop that the jeweller noticed that some of his stock had been exchanged for imitations [See chapter 21 – *What's Tha Up To This Time?*].

The snout had previously agreed with John to meet him at the Cavendish club that night in order to pass on some more information, but unfortunately someone had obviously got to him first.

It later transpired that the two arrested men had loads of convictions for violence, including a couple of shootings. They were obviously professional 'enforcers' and once more they were later sent back to the slammer (prison).

Gone now was my hope of a quiet night shift. I was left standing at the bar finishing my pint, thinking about the mountain of paper work I had to clear up back at the office. So, after downing my drink, I headed back to the 'nick'.

As I drove out of the city, heading towards the M1 motorway and Attercliffe, I shuddered as I remembered when I myself had been savagely beaten up by a gang of lads a few months before I'd joined the Sheffield City Police Force as a 19-year-old in 1962. At that time I was a blacksmith and therefore a big and powerful chap, but not powerful enough to stop the knuckle dusters and bike chains bouncing off my body and head. Some of the lumps and scars are still there today. Before I was allowed to join the police I had to have a medical examination with Professor Alan Usher, the police pathologist. He could see that I was in a bit of a mess as I still had scabs and cuts from the beating; and as he felt at one of the lumps at the base of my skull where the first blow from the knuckle duster had hit me, he said, 'If that blow there Johnson had hit you a quarter of an inch to the left you would have been as dead as a dodo, you've been a lucky lad.' It really hit home to me how close I had been to snuffing it and I'll never forget his words.

Back at the soot-covered Victorian police station at Whitworth Lane, I climbed the stairs up to the CID office. First things first, pint-pot of tea and a fag. There was a message on my desk to give Ken, the security man at Sheffield's wholesale fish market, a call. I thought I knew what he wanted and sure enough I was right.

The market was a large complex containing lots of wholesale florists, greengrocers and dealers of fresh fish. It was surrounded on all sides by a long, sloping grass embankment, at the top of which was a concrete, slatted fence surmounted by barbed wire which encircled the whole area. The only way in or out was via the large front double gates, in the middle of which was the nightwatchman's cabin.

On odd occasions over the last week or two, large pieces of fish had been taken from open-topped boxes full of fish packed in ice, which had been left outside the various fishmongers' shops, having been delivered and dropped off by Tony Alexander from Aberdeen. Tony was the daft bugger who nicked my police car in my book *What's Tha Up To?* The boxes had been left on a delivery dock outside the dozen or so fishmongers' shops. The concrete dock itself was about four feet off the ground and approached from either end by a concrete ramp.

I gave Ken a call and he asked that if I had an hour to spare could I join him and his dog at about 4 am to have a look round the market in order to try and catch the perpetrators of the heinous crime – 'nicking fish'. This was a first for me and if the lads back at the nick knew that I was looking for a fish thief they would have laughed their heads off. We had staked it out twice before and had not come up with anything; there was no way in and no way out without Ken being able to see them. So how was it being stolen? It remained a complete mystery.

On arrival at the market I could see Ken talking to Tony who was just about to leave for his long journey back to Aberdeen. I could see that both of them were in serious conversation, which was totally out of character for them both.

'Martyn, I've just checked every bit of fish in them boxes and every single one is okay. The fishmongers are saying that I am leaving short measures but I'm not. If the buggers aren't caught soon it's going to cost me a lot of business. Fish is not cheap at this time of year and I could lose some customers,' explained Tony.

'Like you Tony I haven't got a clue and neither has Ken. All we can do is stake it out again for the third time and let's see what happens; other than that I'm stumped,' I replied.

Tony drove off and left Ken and me scratching our heads.

It was now only an hour before the market opened. We knew the fish had recently been dropped off and had been thoroughly checked. So whoever was stealing the fish had only an hour left before the shopkeepers would be arriving to open up shop.

Ken kept his German Shepherd dog on a short lead and between us we could see from a distance of about 30 to 40 yards the whole of one side of the fish dock; and we quietly watched in the shadows as dawn was breaking.

For the first half hour we didn't see or hear anything untoward; and then suddenly as I glanced at the concrete ramp furthest away from me, I got the shock of my life. There, walking nonchalantly up the ramp, came both a dog fox and a vixen; and to me as a country lad born and bred, the sight left me spellbound. Old 'Charlie' was followed by his 'missis' – the vixen – and then, unbelievably, three fox cubs. Fox cubs are usually born towards the middle of March and are kept under ground in their 'earth' as a safety measure for about two months; and it looked to me as if this could be one of their first family outings together.

As Ken and I watched in disbelief they slowly trotted along the unloading dock in full view of both us and Ken's dog. Both adults picked up a large piece of fish, almost as big as themselves, and one of the cubs cheekily followed suit and picked up a smaller fish from a separate box which looked, to me, a bit like a 'flat fish'. I was absolutely gob smacked – if only I'd got a camera. At this point they casually walked off down to the other end of the fish dock itself and turned right towards the sloping bank, 20 to 30 yards in front of us – all in a line just like 'follow my leader'. To say I was astounded would be an understatement and if I hadn't seen the next thing that happened with my own eyes I would never have believed it. However, both Ken and I can assure you that what happened next was completely true.

By now the German Shepherd had seen the foxes and the foxes had also seen us but did not look in the least bit concerned. The dog was on a long lead by this stage and we were walking fairly fast towards the foxes. Ken slipped the dogs lead and released him just as the foxes got to the bottom of the tall grassy slope. The foxes, in a line, trotted halfway up the slope, turned left and performed a large circle on the grass before coming back down the same path that they had just run up.

What are they doing? I thought, the Alsatian will rip them to bits. At that point they were back on the tarmac where they then turned right and away to our left. The dog had them in full view but instead of CHASING the foxes themselves he followed the SCENT TRAIL left by them. Barking as he went, he ran part way up the grassy bank and turned left, completing a circle just as the foxes had done before him. Then, miraculously, instead of turning left out of the circle, the dog kept on following the scent of the foxes and ran round and round the circle that they had made.

Ken and I were speechless and eventually Ken had to go up the slope and grab hold of the dog's collar or he would still have been going round and round in circles. It was amazing to see. The foxes, with their young cubs, had gone along with the fish that they had stolen. Later on we found a small break at the base of one of the concrete slats that crafty Charlie the fox and his family had got through. It was their own private entrance and exit.

Poor old Ken went barmy at the dog who, even though he had seen the foxes, followed their scent instead; and there is no doubt whatsoever in our minds that crafty Charlie knew exactly what he was doing. He and his cubs were hungry and that night, at least, they ate better than I did (potted meat sandwiches and a banana for me).

A couple of nights later Ken and I met Tony when he arrived from Aberdeen and he could not believe what had happened.

All three of us were laughing our heads off at the thoughts of it all; and that at last we knew who had stolen the fish. He later arranged with the individual fishmongers to have a key to their premises and from then on the fish was left inside.

A few nights after this I was off duty and went for a pint with my good friend Harry Gale, the well-respected head gamekeeper of Earl Fitzwilliam. I couldn't wait to tell him the story. I casually related the tale to Harry, who then amazed me by saying, 'I can't understand why you are so surprised, Martyn. Us humans think we're clever, lad, but take it from me they don't call old Charlie the crafty fox for nothing – they knew just what they were doing. They can certainly run rings round us!' and we both laughed.

I'll never forget that night. One minute I was dealing with what could easily have been a murder and then the next thing I was chasing a family of crafty foxes nicking fish. It was all part of the job; and yet again reinforced the point that with a job like ours you never knew what was going to happen next.

CHAPTER 2

How Would *You* React?

The M1 south-bound was quiet as I headed towards Attercliffe and work. Even though it was a sunny Sunday afternoon I could still see plenty of smoke belching out from the many steelworks in the area.

Back in the 1960s, Sheffield was still the steel and cutlery capital of the world and many thousands of people depended on the output of the steel melting furnaces in order for them to make a living. This section of the motorway had not been open long, and because of this, the lack of traffic made it a sheer pleasure to drive on. I was just musing to myself about how life was now very different to when I joined the job as a young rookie; and I was thinking about how naive I was when I first joined the police force at the age of nineteen. From the small coal mining village of Darfield near Barnsley I arrived in the big city of Sheffield and wondered what had hit me. There were so many people, so many cars and so many lessons to be learnt. Now, eight years later, here I was working as a detective. A lot of water had gone under the bridge during those few years.

Aye, Aye – what the bloody hell … I thought, as an old car with L plates on and travelling very, very slowly, suddenly veered from the slow lane, into the middle lane and then back into the slow lane again. I had to quickly switch lanes myself and moved into the middle lane, which was fortunately empty, and then, looking through my side windows as I came alongside the car I could see two Asian men, one in the driver's seat and one in the passenger seat. The man in the passenger seat was holding the steering wheel with his right hand. What the hell is going off here? I thought.

I slowed down and at this point saw that the car to my left was in the process of turning left onto the slip road to leave the motorway at Meadowbank, just as I was about to do myself. Looking to my left again, I was amazed to see that the passenger appeared to be giving the driver instructions.

Because it was so hot, both our car windows were partially open and, even though I wasn't in uniform, I peeped the horn on my car, put my warrant card to the window, shouted 'Police!' and told the man to pull over onto the hard shoulder, which he duly did.

I knew that there was an L plate on the back of 'the car. I parked my car on the hard shoulder with its hazard lights on and walked to the front of the old car and noted that there was an L plate on the front *as well as* the back. The driver's window was fully down now and I could see that he was terrified, as I once more showed my warrant card.

The passenger of the car got out and, as I spoke to him, I could see that he was also shaking after realizing that I was a police officer.

'Am I right in thinking that you are teaching this man to drive on the motorway?' I shouted, in shocked amazement.

'Yes sir. This bit of road sir, is very quiet and straight so I thought I would give my friend a driving lesson,' he replied.

'You've got to be joking. This is a motorway and is only available to competent motorists who have already passed their test.' When I said this I could see that both men were visibly shaken by what I had told them.

'Sir, I am very, very sorry. I do not know that law or I would not have done it. It is my friend's first driving lesson and with the road being so straight and quiet I thought it would be a good place to start,' he explained.

I reported them and very quickly took both their details; and told the passenger of the car to drive off the slip road immediately. Luckily there were no vehicles about and so I arranged with them for me to call and see them later at their nearby homes. Both men had been very polite and I could see that they genuinely didn't know that they were committing an offence.

I continued on to work shaking my head in total disbelief. Thank goodness they hadn't caused an accident or the outcome would have been very different.

By the time I got to work Rick and John, my team mates, had already mashed. Rick was checking his crime diary whilst John was on the telephone. I grabbed a pint pot of tea, an ash tray and joined them in the office. Paperwork was the bane of our lives – we were detectives, not typists and looking at the callouses at the end of each of my forefingers told me that I would never make a typist anyway – what a balls-aching job. At that point the phone went so I picked it up and said, 'Detective Constable Johnson.' It was Sergeant Dennis Hoyland in the downstairs office, who surprised me by saying, 'There's a prisoner on his way to the nick Martyn – can you deal with him?'

'Why Dennis, what's up?'

'A bloke's just caught his 10-year-old daughter being indecently assaulted by a 'scum bag' up near the canal on Tinsley Park Road,' he replied. 'He's on his way to the nick with him now.'

'Okay Dennis, give me a ring when he gets here,' I said; and with that I lit a fag and finished my pot of tea while the going was good.

After ten minutes I suddenly realized that surely the arrested man should be here by now. It was only a quarter of a mile away. So where had they got to?

I went downstairs to the main office just in time to see the double doors of the police station crash open and a bloke being thrown through them, the man landing face down on the floor. At the same time a big burly bloke with his shirt sleeves rolled up bellowed, 'Somebody come and sort this dirty bastard out before I rip his head off. He's just indecently assaulted my daughter.'

'Where's your daughter now mate? Is she ok?' I asked.

'My missus has taken her back home and I brought him here,' he said, pointing to the man on the floor. 'He's lucky I didn't drown the bastard in the canal.'

The chap on the floor looked as though he'd done ten rounds with Cassius Clay. Both his eyes were closed and it looked as though he had one or two of his teeth missing. (What a shame, I thought. If he'd indecently assaulted my own daughter he'd be in a far worse state than that.)

'How's he got these injuries mate?' I asked the bloke (and secretly hoped that his reply to me would not be too incriminating).

'As I was dragging him to the station he somehow kept falling on the floor,' he replied, somewhat unconvincingly. 'It looks as though he unfortunately landed on his face a few times!' he concluded, giving me a knowing look.

That reply will do for me, I inwardly thought. None of us liked people who indecently assault children and I had to, very delicately, make sure that there wasn't going to be a complaint of assault made about the father of the little girl concerned.

The man's injuries were far from life threatening and when I asked him if he had any complaints to make about the girl's father there was a pause. Through his swollen eyes he looked first at the father, who with clenched fists was glaring at him, and then at me and simply said, 'No!'

When asked, the man declined hospital treatment and at that point I placed him in a cell – time now to go and see the little girl; with the complainant being a female and also a juvenile, I asked Pat, one of the policewomen, to conduct the interview with her and, along with the girl's father, we walked the short distance to their home on Broughton Lane, near to where the incident had taken place.

On arrival at the house I got a bit of a shock. Mum was in the living room comforting her daughter who was crying. I instantly recognized her as being one of the little girls I used to take across the road when she was on her way to the Doctor Worrall Special School on Maltby Street. The reason that I remembered her so well was that she was a pretty little blond-haired girl and no matter whenever I saw her at school or whilst I was working my beat she always wore the biggest smile you had ever seen. She was a sweet little child who smiled at everybody but who was, unfortunately, of low intellect, having a mental age of a five-year-old.

When interviewed by Pat, it appeared that mum and dad, along with little Sarah, had taken a picnic up to the canal, it being such a lovely sunny day.

Whilst dad was 'splodging' (fishing) little Sarah went to play nearby with some other girls. At some point she'd been approached by the man who offered her some sweets. He then took her behind a bush, put his hand over her mouth, pulled down her knickers and started to fondle her. Fortunately, one of her little playmates went to find her, saw what was happening and started to scream. At that point the dirty man started to run away; but unfortunately for him he was running in the direction of where Sarah's dad was fishing. Sarah also started to scream and when dad jumped up and saw her with her knickers round her ankles he realized what had happened; and caught the man, wrestling him to the floor.

Another fisherman had also seen what was happening and it was he who had run to the telephone box; and rung to tell us that the two men were on their way to the police station.

Poor little Sarah and her mum and dad were beside themselves. She was their only child and now that lovely little smile was gone.

It's a bit of a bugger when a loving family can't even take their little defenceless daughter for a picnic without some mindless, evil monster attacking her in such a way. Having the mental age of a 5-year-old, and quite rightly and understandably not knowing any better, she'd trusted the man.

As Pat, the policewoman, coaxed the story about what had happened from Sarah, I noticed that her dad's fists were bunched up, just as mine were. I realized that both of us were pacing up and down in frustration and anger as I am sure that you yourself would have been when faced with the same circumstances.

Pat and I later walked back to the police station to where I was going to interview Mr Dirty Bastard himself. I was absolutely livid and was certainly not well disposed to the evil 'pillock' that I had left in the cells; to such a degree that before I got him out of the cell I had to ask an inspector to sit with me during the interview as I seriously wanted to smash him to a pulp.

As I write this nearly fifty years after that incident I can still see little Sarah's face without its lovely smile and ask 'why?' It makes me angry all over again.

Under interview I obtained the man's details and ran them through the National Crime Intelligence Unit. Surprise, surprise, our Mr Dirty Bastard was wanted for the rape of a 13-year-old girl which had taken place at the side of a canal near Worksop about 18 months earlier, only fifteen miles away in Nottinghamshire. During his trial for rape he had apparently jumped out of the dock and through a side door of the court; and he had not been seen since. He had previously lived on a barge on the canal and was strongly suspected of further assaults of young girls on the canal sides as far away as Birmingham and Cheshire. Knowing these facts only made me feel worse and I was getting angrier by the minute.

Sitting opposite me during the interview, I could see that his eyes, although swollen, were dark, emotionless and cold looking and he showed no remorse for his actions whatsoever. At that point I had to wonder what this bloke might have done in the past. Indecent assault on anybody, let alone a child, is bad enough but then to rape a child is another matter altogether. Having been involved in several rape enquiries during my time in the Force I can tell you that the perpetrators are ruthless and capable of anything. Some, after having committed the rape panic and try to strangle the victim in order to avoid recognition. The evil pillock that was sitting opposite to me now, made me realize that little Sarah could well have been lucky to have got away that day.

Nottinghamshire police were contacted and thanked us for the arrest, and they said that they would send someone to come and collect him straight away. Rape was a far more serious offence than our indecent assault, and as the rape had been committed in Nottinghamshire then he would have to go back there to stand trial. If he pleaded guilty or was found guilty of the rape then our offence would be taken into consideration.

Whilst we waited for them to come and fetch him I had to keep going outside to calm myself down or otherwise I might also have ended up in court for what I would have liked to have done, which was quite simple – administer rough justice to some mindless person who was worth neither snap nor 'baccy' (tobacco). The Nottinghamshire police duly arrived, handcuffed him and took him away; and he must have pleaded guilty because I was never called upon to give evidence. I'm certain that he must have been sent to prison for a long time. I'll never forget his evil face and neither will I ever forget young Sarah's smile. It's not in my nature to get angry and uptight; normally I am very placid and sometimes as daft as a brush but when you see the look of terror on an innocent child's face and the tears that go with it you can't help but let your own emotions get to you – after all we are only human.

Now that I'm older I have been given to understand that there are over twenty organizations set up to help the perpetrators of crime and only one to assist the victims. What a stupid and barmy world we live in – where's it all gone wrong?

By this time I was so wound up that I decided to call in for a beer and a game of crib with the lads in the Mason's Arms at Thorpe Hesley, near to where I lived. I grabbed a pint and went into the tap room where Les, Harry and Wilf were sitting at the long Formica-topped table, obviously looking for someone to make a 'four up' at crib.

Les looked up at me and said, 'Bloody hell Martyn, tha's a face like a busted clog. What's up wi thee?'

Harry said, 'I've seen him like this afore, dunt upset him Les, tha might end up wi' a clout.' Whilst Wilf, being the gentleman he was, who would normally curse me if we were losing at crib, tactfully said, 'Come and sit down lad. We'll win these two dozy buggers tonight.' And sure enough, two hours later, I was 8p up. It made a change for Wilf and I to win, but more importantly the laughter and banter between us all had released the anger and frustration brought about by the day's events, and when I got home I slept like a log.

CHAPTER 3

When's a Jewel Not a Jewel?

The following day – Monday – saw Christine and myself up bright and early with glorious sunshine beaming in through the windows of our house. What a cracking day, I was glad to be alive. After breakfast we decided to put Richard, our son who was only a few months old, into his pram and take him for a walk before I set off to work at 3.00pm. I treasured times like this when the three of us would go out for a stroll in the early morning and I knew just where I was heading for.

As a youngster growing up in the village of Darfield I always headed out towards the woods and the river where I would spend hours and hours on my own just observing the wildlife going on around me. The peace and quiet of the countryside, with just the bird sounds for company was bliss for me. I couldn't wait for my little lad to grow older in order that I could teach him as much about nature as possible. Up until the age of seven I had no playmates as we lived at the bottom of Vicar Lane right next to the river Dearne with only two elderly neighbours on either side. My only 'playmates' were the animals, birds, frogs, beetles and insects. In my first years at school I was always top of the class in nature studies but in everything else I was always bottom – unfortunately for me nothing has changed since those early days, I hated school.

Christine and I eventually walked into the woods. It was great, the birds were singing their little heads off which was lovely to hear. It was the time of year when most birds had had their first clutch of youngsters and watching and listening to them along with the sight of an odd rabbit or two made me realize just how lucky we were. Attercliffe, where I worked, was only about three miles from where we lived but because of the pollution, when the birds sang there, their voices sounded as though they were on forty fags a day, poor things.

Later on and back at home we had dinner and then Christine packed up my snap ready for work. Cold fish sandwiches with a touch of tomato sauce, along with the obligatory two bananas suited me fine. Christine couldn't understand why I liked cold fish sandwiches but I just loved them and still do today. At 2.30pm I once more set off down the M1 and couldn't help chuckling to myself in disbelief about the antics of the Asian man trying to teach his mate to drive on the motorway.

Thinking of this reminded me that I needed to see my good friend Mr Dar, the tailor, as he had telephoned to let me know that my new suit was ready to be collected. So when I got to work I signed on duty at 3.00pm and then nipped round to his shop which was only fifty yards away on the corner of Old Hall Road and Fell Road. All our lads, as well as many more people in Sheffield, used Mr Dar when wanting a made-to-measure suit. He was excellent at his job and also cheaper than other tailors.

As I approached the shop I could see his young son, who I nicknamed 'Freddie', sitting near to his dad who was, as usual, sewing away. I'd helped to teach young Freddie to read and write when the family first arrived from Pakistan about eight years earlier. The Dar family were all lovely people and I knew that the first thing that Mrs Dar would do was go and make me a cup of tea which she made with milk for some reason.

Walking into the shop I could see that Mr Dar was talking to another chap and I was quite surprised to see that it was the same man who had been driving the car, under tuition, on the M1 the day before. When he turned and saw me he nearly passed out with fear. At this point Mr Dar introduced me to the man and explained that he was his nephew and that he'd called in to tell his uncle about what had happened on the motorway the day before. When Mr Dar realized that I was the bloke who'd reported his nephew he sent him out of the shop to go and fetch the other man concerned, who turned out to be a friend of his. Brilliant, I thought, that will save me going to see them at their homes as I had previously arranged to do the day before.

Mr Dar, who by then knew what had happened on the motorway, started to talk to them both in a loud voice. Even though I couldn't understand the language, which was probably Urdu, it was obvious from their faces that they were getting a rollicking from Mr Dar. They were both looking down at the floor like naughty children and were nodding their heads and fidgeting all at the same time and their faces looked as forlorn as a turkey at Christmas. On three separate occasions during Mr Dar's tirade both men suddenly turned, looked at me and in stilted English, simultaneously said, 'Sorry Mr Johnson.' (Which made me chuckle.)

By the time that Mr Dar had finished his telling off, and because of his stern face, I was nearly as jittery as they were and nearly said, 'Sorry Mr Dar,' when he'd done. It sounded and also looked to me that both men had learned a lesson, and neither I nor a magistrate could have done a better job than Mr Dar had presumably done – they looked like naughty little school boys waiting for the cane.

Mr Dar explained to me that neither men had realized that they were doing wrong, which in a way was understandable as prior to that section of the motorway opening the M1 used to start/finish south of Sheffield. Both their driving documents were in order and therefore I became judge and jury. It seemed to me that in this case it would be more prudent to foster better understanding and promote good public relations rather than to send them both to court.

When I conveyed the news to them that they weren't going to court both of them shook my hand and thanked me profusely. Job done – everybody happy! With that I finished my milky tea, thanked Mr and Mrs Dar and went back to the office.

As I got to the top of the stairs leading to the CID office my team-mate Rick shouted, 'Where the bloody hell as tha been and what's tha been up to?'

'Why, Rick. What's up?' I said, 'I've only been gone three-quarters of an hour.'

'Superintendent Barker's been looking for you. He's in his office and he wants to see you. But I haven't a clue as to why.'

What the hell does he want I thought? You might see a superintendent once a year, if you were unlucky that is. They were like gods in those days and they stayed in their office and were rarely seen. I lit a fag and sat down to take stock. I couldn't think what he wanted me for at all. I mulled things over to try and think if I'd done something wrong but couldn't bring anything to mind. I finished my fag and stood up, looked out of the window on to the not so clean street below and thought well I might as well get this over with; and so with trepidation I went downstairs to his office and knocked on the door.

'Who is it?' a voice shouted from within.

'Detective Constable Johnson, Sir,' I said; and even though I was 'bricking it' I tried to sound as confident as possible.

'Argh. Come in Johnson.'

I entered his office and as he sat there behind his desk he said, 'I've been looking for you Johnson. Sit down.'

I did as I was told and breathed a sigh of relieve as it seemed that I wasn't in trouble this time. Picking up a sheet of paper from his desk he looked at me and said, 'Does the name Mary ----- mean anything to you?'

'Not that I can recall, Sir, no,' I answered.

'I've got a memo here from the Chief Constable himself making enquiries about a policeman with a strong Barnsley accent who gave the 'kiss of life' to a young girl about four years ago,' he explained.

I thought for a moment and suddenly recalled young Mary who I had, indeed, given the 'kiss of life' to [see Chapter 18, *What's Tha Up To Nah?*].

'Yes, Sir. If she lives at 'such and such' address then that would be me, Sir. Is something wrong?' I asked.

He must have seen the worried expression on my face, smiled and said, 'No lad, no. It's the opposite. A lady called Sadie has written to the Chief Constable saying that her daughter Mary would like to invite you to her 21st birthday party as a thank you for saving her life – well done lad, well done!' he said and he passed over the details to me. I could see from Sadie's address that it was the right one. I was absolutely astounded.

'If it is you, then the Chief Constable sends his congratulations as well,' he concluded; and with that I left his office and went back upstairs in a daze, mashed a pot of tea and lit a fag. Bloody hell that's a first, I thought, I couldn't get over it. Looking at the details on the memo told me that the party was in a couple of weeks' time and at that point I suddenly realized that the suit I'd gone to fetch from Mr Dar was still there. With all the talk of the motorway incident and Mr Dar's connection to the two blokes involved I'd completely forgotten what I'd gone for. I was getting dozier by the day.

I didn't have time to muse on the situation for long as Inspector Hepworth asked me to go to see a business man in the Firth Park area who had reported the theft of jewellery from his car, so I grabbed a car key, jumped into the Morris Minor (one of the CID cars) and off I went; my new suit would have to wait.

As I drove up the hill and through Grimesthorpe I could see Ronnie [see Chapter 20 – *What's Tha Up To?*] waiting outside the police box. You usually found him at this time of day waiting there for the policeman who was designated to work the school crossing. Ronnie would don his white coat and loved to help to take the children across the road from school.

I pulled up for a quick chat with Ronnie and when he saw me his face lit up.

'Martyn – miss you, Martyn – miss you,' Ronnie said.

Ronnie, who at that time would be about 55 years old had had severe learning difficulties all his life and we all took time out to make him feel a bit special, which he was to us. He was a lovely chap and had always wanted to be a policeman and help take the children across the road to school near to where he lived. Between some of our lads we had managed to scrounge him a white traffic coat and bits of uniform including a helmet which were kept in the old police box, outside of which he was now standing. We all loved Ronnie and whichever policeman was on duty would stop the traffic in order for the children to cross the road; and then Ronnie would join him in the middle of the road with his hands in the air just like the policeman; Ronnie loved it, we loved it, the kids loved it, motorists loved it and no one ever complained. Imagine that happening today! The police force was very different back in those days – for the better in my opinion! It was more personal – something which we bobbies were all proud to be a part of.

I drove down through Page Hall and through Fir Vale towards the Firth Park area of the city, which even then was a pretty rough area to police, but certainly nowhere near as bad as it is today.

I pulled up at the address I'd been given and couldn't believe my eyes. It was a dental practice, something that I dreaded.

Prior to me being instructed to join the CID I'd quite happily worked the beat in uniform and loved it. It was to me the most satisfying job in the world – meeting people like Ronnie, taking the kids across the road to school, chatting to all the shop keepers and old people. It wasn't work to me at all – it was a pleasure and I was missing it terribly. After eighteen months as a detective I'd realized that I much preferred to work the beat and be with the local people. Being a detective was a great experience but not as fulfilling or satisfying as working with the local community.

Inevitably on a job like ours where you never knew what was going to happen next, you'd get involved in scraps and during the previous eight years I'd lost several teeth on different occasions through fighting which had caused me some considerable pain. At one time when I opened my mouth my teeth must have looked like a set of garden railings. I was getting uglier by the day; and every time I lost another the dentist would have to make me another pallet; dentists weren't my favourite people, I'd rather tackle ten men with a knife a piece.

Walking in through the front door I could see two nervous looking people in the waiting room and so I introduced myself to the receptionist. She informed the dentist that I had arrived and he poked his head round the corner and beckoned me into the surgery where a poor bloke was in the chair with his mouth wide open. Bloody hell fire, I thought, let me get out of here. I told the dentist that I'd wait in the waiting room until he had dealt with all his patients, which I duly did; but I also kept nipping out for a quick fag. Half an hour later all three patients had left and so we sat down for a chat.

'Mr Toothpuller' told me that at lunch time he had nipped out in his car to buy a sandwich and also to put some money into the bank – at which point I inadvertently chuckled. As I did so he looked at me rather quizzically and wondered why I had laughed.

'Sorry,' I replied 'it must be my Barnsley sense of humour. Normally you people are taking things out and when you told me you were putting things in I saw the funny side. Sorry, please continue.'

'When I got back to my car I found that the back window had been smashed and my briefcase had been stolen. I was mortified,' he said.

'Oh dear, what was in the case?' I asked. When I asked that question the bloke looked around to check whether there was anybody within earshot and quietly said to me, 'I am a Freemason.'

'Oh,' I replied; and for some stupid reason I also whispered.

The only thing that I knew about the freemasons at that time was that they were a secret society and a powerful group of people who helped others. I couldn't understand why he was whispering but asked him to continue.

'The briefcase contains my masonic regalia including the jewels that we wear and also some books which are very precious,' he explained.

As he said the words 'jewels and precious' my ears pricked up and my imagination ran riot as I imagined a case full of jewellery. 'Wow,' I said, 'it's not every day that we get a jewellery theft in our division. Have you got a photograph of them?'

'Sorry – no I haven't,' he replied.

I took a statement from him, listing the stolen items; and when I asked him to put a value on them he quite simply said, 'They're priceless and irreplaceable!'

I'd already asked the fingerprint lads to attend to check for any 'dabs' that the thief might have left on the car but they couldn't find anything at all. As I left the dental practice to start my enquiries I could envisage the headlines in the *Sheffield Star*, 'PRICELESS JEWELS STOLEN FROM CAR'.

By this time all the pawnbroker shops and second-hand shops in the area were closed as it was early evening, otherwise I would have checked there and then whether they had been offered any 'priceless jewels'. So I went back to the office and typed up a report; but I couldn't stop thinking about the word *jewels* and *priceless;* and the fact that he couldn't put a price on the stolen items.

Where could I start my enquiries at this time of night?

Suddenly I thought about a pal of mine called Henry who, at that time, worked in the steelworks but during his leisure time he would call in at different pubs and buy jewellery and watches off anybody who happened to be 'skint'. He would then add a small profit and sell them on to anyone who wanted them. Henry had been born in the Caribbean but had lived in Sheffield from an early age. He was an absolutely brilliant bloke, kind, caring and comical. He was as straight as a die and he would never buy anything off anybody if he suspected that it was stolen. He used to drive a little three-wheeler car, just like Del Boy of *Only Fools and Horses*; the difference was that his vehicle was blue rather than yellow.

Henry used the pubs all over the city and beyond but mainly in the Pitsmoor, Burngreave and Firth Park areas of the city; so it was quite possible that he might just have been offered the jewellery for sale. It was worth a try – so off I went to try and find him.

I called into one or two pubs and in the end bumped into Basil, one of Henry's pals who told me that I would catch him in the Prospect Tavern at Hoyland near Barnsley where he went on a Monday evening. Sure enough, as I went into the pub there he was, laughing his head off as usual, what a great guy. He shook my hand vigorously and bought me a pint. We went into a quiet part of the pub and I told him the story of the dentist who'd had his masonic jewellery stolen; and the fact that the guy said that the jewellery was priceless, which to me, meant that it was worth thousands of pounds. At that point Henry started to chuckle.

'Why are you laughing Henry? I've got to solve this crime,' I said.

'Martyn, the majority of masonic jewellery is only made of base metal. On rare occasions some pieces may be silver but rarely of gold. They are called masonic jewels which, to a Freemason, is symbolic of a jewel rather than being a proper jewel with high value. That's why he said that they were priceless. Meaning that they were priceless to him but not to anyone else.'

What Henry had said suddenly made sense and I felt a right dope and had to laugh to myself. I later checked up with a pal of mine who I knew was a Freemason and he told me exactly the same as Henry. It just shows you how you can get things wrong.

Once every few weeks we had a CID conference where all detectives got together to discuss any problematic cases that they were currently dealing with and if I hadn't clarified with Henry, my mate, as to the proper value of the medals, which was minimal, I would have spoken at the conference about the 'priceless medals', making me look a right 'tea cake'. I had to assume that some of our high-ranking officers were probably freemasons themselves, which would have made them chuckle if I'd mentioned the word priceless. Little was I to know then that a good few years after this incident I myself would learn more about freemasonry.

I had a couple of quick pints with Henry and scuttled off home to bed. Ah well! We're never too old to learn. What a twerp!

CHAPTER 4

Bottoms Up

'The f_____ bastard. I can't take any more of this,' she cried. Tears were streaming down her face and mascara ran down her cheeks. Her right eye was swollen and blood was dripping from her nose and into her ample cleavage. She looked totally different to when I'd last seen her a couple of hours before, when she was touting for business as a prostitute in the Wicker in the centre of Sheffield.

I always remember, it was a Thursday evening and my partner in the CID for that day was Ricky Hardwick. We were both on afternoons, the 3pm to 11pm shift, and we'd earlier arrested a couple of rough lads for breaking into cars and stealing the contents. They had readily admitted the jobs and we'd taken them up to the charge office at police headquarters, Water Lane, where they would spend a night in the cold cells (how sad!) before their court appearance the following day. Unfortunately the cars they'd broken into didn't include Mr Toothpuller's car and his stolen jewels.

Sheffield was full of pubs and some of them, like the one we were now in, were beer-only pubs and not allowed to sell spirits. Being in the back streets of the tough East End of the city meant that it was normally quiet and didn't attract many outsiders. We always looked forward to visiting the pub as it was full of characters, as you no doubt have read about in *What's Tha Up To This Time?* Most of the works surrounding the pub were closed for the evening and as we drove down the cobbled street the odd gas lamp shone onto the snow-covered road and pavement.

We pulled up at the side of the red telephone box which was situated just outside the pub. It had a pane of glass missing from one of its side windows and every time I saw it, it made me chuckle. The phone box itself was referred to as the 'outside office' by the usual customers who used the pub.

As we entered the pub we knew what would happen when we got inside and sure enough it did. 'ONE, TWO, THREE, CID,' shouted the men in the snug and one of the lads affectionately known as 'Soft Cock' shouted across the room in an effeminate voice to Cecil the bar man, 'Two halves for those two gorgeous men.' And he blew us a kiss – now you know what I meant when I said that the pub was full of characters.

It was almost like being in someone's house when you went in. There was a small room on the left and a large room to the right, with a passageway leading to the backyard and the outside toilets. If I went into the pub on my own or with Rick and John, it was always the same: 'ONE, TWO, THREE, CID' and someone would buy us our first drink which was always a half. If we'd have supped a pint in every pub we visited we'd have been pie-eyed after an hour or two – so we stuck to halves.

The regular lads (or 'queens') were in the snug, including George, whose long blonde wig was on the bar as usual. Looking into the bigger room I could see more regulars, including the two grey-haired old black men with dominoes in one hand and dancing to the calypso music coming from the juke box. How they did that I will never know. How can you dance and play dominoes at the same time? There was a roaring fire, most welcome on a snowy night like this, and one or two of the girls were standing in front of it warming their arses. Just like the men in the snug, the girls were always the same when they saw us, pouting their lips and sticking out their boobs, shouting 'Are you looking for business, big boy?'

This was our pub of choice if we wanted to relax and have a good laugh. They were a great bunch of people. Sadly it was knocked down many years ago. We'd not been in the place five minutes when through the door you could hear the phone ringing in the telephone box outside and Cecil, the barman, nipped outside to take the call. As he came back in, shivering from the cold, with an effeminate voice he said, 'Phone for you Denise.' Denise then left the pub. Within a minute she was back inside, 'Client at the flat, see you back here in an hour. Bye,' she shouted to the girls as she was leaving the pub and at the same time she stuck out her chest; and purposely brushed her breasts against me as she went out.

Thirty seconds later I heard the phone ring again but Cecil was busy pulling a pint, so with a chuckle I went outside and answered. It had certainly got colder, so I walked quickly back into the pub and shouted to George, 'George – one for you.'

'Thanks Mr Johnson,' he said as he minced past me and went to the telephone kiosk, coming back in shortly afterwards.

'That's two you've had tonight,' said one of the lads in the snug; 'when is it my turn?' George grabbed his coat and at the same time put his long blonde wig on his shaven head and blew Rick and me a kiss as he left the pub.

What a place and what characters!

Rick had first taken me into this pub some eighteen months previously and I wondered what had hit me. For whatever reason you were always guaranteed a good laugh to such a degree that my wife Christine and Rick's wife Doreen were always asking if they could go into the pub to see for themselves what it was like. They pestered us so much that one night we took them in.

The lads in the snug bought them a drink each, the girls in the main room brought them stools to sit on (Christine, was heavily pregnant with our second child) and they were entertained by the two black men. Not one swear word was uttered that night and at one point I turned round and couldn't believe my eyes when Doreen and Christine were playing dominoes in front of the fire and tapping their feet in time with the music.

The pub has to rank as the best and most relaxed pub that I have ever been in and the girls thought it was brilliant. I wish it was still here. What a laugh and what an education.

At times it could be a little bit confusing when some of the lads, for reasons known only to them, used girls' names as well; and as the immaculately dressed landlady (Mary) used to say, 'I know what most of them do for a living, and that's up to them, but they don't cause any problems to anybody in here because they know they'll be barred if they do.'

Over time I got to know them all well (I know what you're thinking, but not that well!). Usually from Thursday onwards if we were in, the lads would buy us a glass of beer; but on Monday, Tuesday and Wednesday when business was poor and they were all skint, then we would buy some of them half a pint of beer. What I liked about the place was that they were all very protective towards each other. Their clients had been given the telephone number of the kiosk outside if they wanted to do 'business'. In other words, their clients knew where to find them. As they said themselves they were safer waiting for business in the pub rather than walking the streets looking for it, especially on a night like tonight when it was freezing cold.

On this occasion we had only been in the place some fifteen minutes when in walked the girl with the bloody nose. Like most of the other girls she was a 'looker' all right. I'd seen her knocking about but I'd never seen her in the pub before. Within minutes the other girls took her into the back room, cleaned her up and calmed her down.

Apparently, and unlike most of the other girls, she (Marlene) was in the clutches of a pimp who was English and also, oddly enough, called Martin. She used to work as a prostitute in the docks area of Lowestoft and for some reason or other she had decided to move to Sheffield where she got involved with the pimp. Whatever money she earned from prostitution was taken off her by Martin who also ran three other girls. They were only allowed to keep enough money for food and work clothes whilst he lived a decent lifestyle on their immoral earnings. Not content with that he also used to beat them all on a regular basis and Marlene couldn't get away from him.

Thankfully, Marlene wasn't badly hurt and half an hour later she left the pub to go back to work the streets once more. If she didn't earn any money she would probably suffer another beating at the hands of Mr Money Grabber. It made us realize just how vulnerable these girls were when they made a living by working the streets on their own. It's the oldest profession in the world but also one of the most dangerous.

Jenny, one of the older girls, explained to us that this Martin bloke was a nasty piece of work and ruthless with his girls. Ricky and I made a mental note of this and wondered how he would fare when dealing with someone as big as he was. After talking to Jenny I ordered another half and at the same time the door opened to reveal 'Doreen', a male prostitute who worked the pubs in and around the city centre. That's weird, I thought, what's he doing in here? Two strangers within an hour using the pub, so what's going off?' At that point I forgot about it as we continued having a laugh and a bit of banter with the lads in the snug.

Five minutes later the door opened again and in walked a uniformed police sergeant and a constable; blimey, I thought to myself, this is getting weirder by the minute.

Most pubs in those days were visited by the police as a matter of routine. These visits were designed to stop both underage drinking and drinking after time but Mary's, which was a quiet backstreet pub, was not known for any trouble and didn't attract underage drinkers. What made it stranger still was the fact that the two officers who we knew didn't acknowledge us and started to check both rooms of the pub. It later transpired that they thought we were working undercover and didn't want to spoil anything, which is why they didn't speak to us. A couple of minutes later, after having checked the pub, they opened the front door and left. Rick and I looked at each other and wondered what was what so I followed them out to find out what they were looking for.

It turned out that about an hour earlier Doreen had mugged a punter near the Raven public house on Division Street, which was at the other side of the city. The man who had been mugged had used the 'services' of Doreen before and he gave a very good description to the two uniformed lads who were dealing with the job. The sergeant realized from this description that it matched Doreen who they also knew worked around that area and so they decided to look for him. They'd looked in quite a lot of the pubs searching for him and someone had told them that he might have come to Mary's quite a long way from the robbery.

'How much money has he robbed him of?' I asked.

'About £100 in notes,' the sergeant answered.

'Blimey, that's a lot of money. He came into the pub a little while ago and I've not seen him leave. Let's go and have another look for him,' I said. He wasn't in the snug with the other lads and as I looked into the other room I saw that Doreen was wedged into a space behind the juke box, no wonder they had missed him.

'Doreen, come here I want a word with you,' I said; and I took him into the passageway. 'These officers are looking for you because they are saying that you mugged a man on Division Street. Is that right?'

'No Mr Johnson, I wouldn't do that,' he stuttered in his effeminate voice and he was sounding very nervous.

'Why were you hiding behind the jukebox Doreen?' At that point his mouth was opening and closing and he didn't know what to say. 'Doreen, I don't like people who tell me lies. If the money is recovered that will help your case in court, so I am now going to ask you for the last time. Have you robbed this bloke on Division Street? If the answer is no again you and I are going out to the backyard where we might fall out.' And I gave him a knowing look which I knew he understood. I got hold of his left arm and led him down the passageway towards the backyard and just before we got there he blurted it out.

'All right Mr Johnson I've done it, you know I have. Please don't hurt me.'

'I'd no intention of hurting you but you weren't to know that. Now where's the money?'

'Come with me,' he sheepishly said; and he went into the outside toilet with me watching his every move to make sure that he didn't try to escape.

'What the hell is he doing now?' I thought.

He dropped his trousers, bent down, put his hand behind him and then offered me a plastic bag. I nearly dropped bow legged – you didn't need to be a brain surgeon to work out where the plastic bag had come from. I've got to say that because of the nature of his profession I wasn't at all surprised at where he did his banking, it had obviously been taken from his depositary! As is usual at times like this when you are supposed to be serious I couldn't help bursting out in laughter. The uniformed lads had come in looking for a prisoner who they had now got and he'd admitted the offence, all they wanted now was the evidence – there was no way that I was going to touch the bag.

I turned and spoke to the sergeant. 'Sergeant it gives me great pleasure to hand Doreen over to you as your prisoner. You have heard him admit to the offence that you have described and I can only assume that the evidence he has magically produced from nowhere will contain the same amount of money that was stolen.' The wise old sergeant looked at me and also started to laugh. Turning to the constable he was with he said with a big smile on his face, 'Officer this is your prisoner, not mine and I suggest that you and not me take possession of the evidence'; and we all looked at the plastic bag that could be seen dangling between Doreen's rather dirty fingers.

The young policeman's face was a picture but full credit to him as he realized that, as the junior, the buck had been passed on to him and he also started to laugh. Good for him, I thought. If you forget how to laugh there's no point in living. I went back into the pub and borrowed a bigger plastic bag from Mary who, when told the story, went absolutely crackers. Back outside Doreen dropped the bag into the clean and larger one. You could see that it was stuffed with rolled up £1 notes and I am sure that it was all there. The sergeant handcuffed Doreen and led him out through the pub.

Mary saw him and her eyes were wild, 'I've only seen you once before, young man, and you've upset my evening. You are now banned from my pub, I run a good house here – don't come here again,' she called after him. With that he was bundled into the police car. The lads in the snug were making all sorts of comments and Ricky, as usual, was in hysterics and as the prisoner was led out of the door Ricky shouted, 'What an arsehole!' Which set us off laughing all over again.

I've said it before and I'll say it again: you never knew from one minute to the next what you were going to deal with. Just before leaving the pub I raised my glass to the lads in the snug and shouted, 'Bottoms up lads!' and that set them off laughing yet again.

I signed off duty and when I got home I told Christine the story and she also laughed her head off; and we were both still chuckling when we went to bed.

CHAPTER 5

An Emotional Roller Coaster

I just could not stop pacing up and down. Calm down, calm down I kept saying to myself; but I just couldn't help it. The thoughts of it all were just sending me crackers. I made myself another pint pot of tea and lit up yet another fag. Christine had taken Richard out for a walk. I wished they would hurry up back, at least if they were in I would have something to occupy my mind. The more I thought about not thinking about it made it even worse. So even though I wasn't a television fan, I turned on our old black and white set to see if it would take my mind off it and give me something else to think about. Bloody hell, why is it always football when I'm a cricket fan? I asked myself, so I tried one of the other two channels. Colour televisions were available then but we just couldn't afford one.

Football on one, news on two, *Tom and Jerry* on the ITV. After ten minutes I was worn out watching Tom chasing Jerry round and round so switched off the television and found myself once more pacing up and down. I hadn't been as nervous as this since Christine had given birth to young Richard and I knew that fairly soon that experience would be repeated as she was heavily pregnant once more.

Walking out into the small back garden I could see in the distance Hoober Stand and knew that the Rockingham Arms at Wentworth was only a couple of miles away. I could have murdered a pint and a bit of banter with the lads but that would just have to wait. My watch said 3.00pm – another four hours to go. I wished I'd not agreed to go, but having made a promise to do so – that was it – I was duty bound to go.

Just then I heard the phone ring – it was Alec, a young mate of mine who was an antique dealer.

'What time do you want picking up tonight, Martyn?' he asked.

'It shouldn't take us long to get there – about quarter to seven should do it. Okay?'

'Okay. I'll pick you up then,' he replied and with that put the phone down. As the phone went down it reminded me of the reason for my current state of trepidation, which started after I'd spoken to Sadie a couple of weeks ago on the phone.

Sadie had written to the Chief Constable hoping to trace the officer who had dealt with a situation at her home four or five years previously. The only thing she could remember in her panic at the time of the incident was the fact that the officer had a broad Barnsley accent and that is how the police had traced me. I couldn't believe it. On phoning Sadie she explained to me that her daughter would be turning 21 in a couple of weeks' time and she expressed to her mother that she would love it if the policeman who had saved her life could come to her 21st birthday. It was lovely to hear her voice again; she had been a very brave woman on the day of the incident. What a compliment and I'd agreed to go. Sadie told me that Mary (her daughter) didn't know that she'd been in touch with me and it was going to be a surprise on the night.

That was a couple of weeks ago and I'd found it very easy to say yes but as time went on I started to think about the scenario; and started to worry. I love parties but this one was going to be different to any other that I'd been to. On the day in question I remembered that I'd been driving a Panda car in a decent and quiet area of the city and had come across a lady who was standing at the side of the road, waving her arms about hysterically. Jumping out of the police car I'd approached her but she was in such a state that she just couldn't speak so somehow she had to be calmed down in order to find out what the problem was – she was in shock. Something was obviously seriously wrong but I didn't know what, so I gently slapped her cheek which did the trick to some degree and she turned and pointed to a nearby house, the front door of which was open. I raced in through the open front door, not knowing what to expect and turned right into the living room. There was nothing obvious in there and it was the same in the kitchen, so I ran upstairs.

Bathroom: nothing; main bedroom: nothing; middle bedroom: the same; I must have missed something. The door to the box bedroom was open and I ran in. There, lying on top of the covers, on a single bed was the lifeless and completely naked body of a teenage girl of about sixteen to seventeen years of age. She was on her back and in one hand was a photograph of a young man; and I could also see a couple of empty bottles which would have held tablets. Now I knew why the poor woman, obviously her mum, was hysterical.

She had no pulse, but she was still warm so I'd raced down to the car and phoned for an ambulance to attend urgently. I also knew that we were about ten minutes' drive from the ambulance station and by the time they got to the house it could be too late; so I had to take some immediate action.

As I ran back upstairs I'd ripped off my tunic and my mind was racing. It was better to try and fail than not to try at all. No time for text books, just get on with it lad. My own heart was thumping as I gently squeezed the girl's nostrils together with one hand and opened her mouth with the other, then I took in a gulp of air and exhaled into her mouth and then released the pressure on her nostrils. I'd done the same again and again and again and again, and just as I thought that I'd failed there was a cough and a splutter and the girl started to breath by herself. It was a moment I'll never forget and I was euphoric.

We were far from out of the woods though, and I knew that even though she was breathing again I somehow had to keep her awake because the overdose of tablets was doing its job. If the girl had been dead and without oxygen for more than five minutes she could also suffer permanent brain damage. Seconds counted and I shouted to the mother to bring a wet towel – and quickly. I did this for two reasons, one to give her mother something to do and focus her mind, and secondly in the hope that the wet towel would come in handy. When she arrived I explained my predicament to her: 'Your daughter needs to stay awake and I need to man handle her to keep her moving, okay?'

The poor woman was beside herself with worry, which was understandable and, even though I felt awkward because the girl had no clothes on, I picked her up from the bed, stood her on her feet and held her up from behind with both my arms around her waist for support. There was no time for niceties.

'What's her name, love?'

'Mary,' she'd replied.

'What's your name?'

'Sadie,' she answered.

'Sadie, put that cold towel on the back of her neck and then try to move her legs backwards and forwards as though she is walking,' I said.

'Mary, Mary keep awake, don't go to sleep, keep awake,' I kept shouting as we somehow shuffled round the little room together.

The drugs inside her had taken effect and she'd kept lapsing in and out of consciousness. I remembered screaming at her, 'Mary! Mary! Keep awake. Mary, keep awake. Wake up! Wake up!' And every time her body sagged and went unconscious again I got Sadie to splash cold water on to her face in the hope that it would shock her into waking up a bit.

As the ambulance had arrived, Mary was groaning a bit which meant that she was alive and still with us. I'd escorted the ambulance at great speed to the Northern General hospital and on our arrival they'd rushed Mary straight into the recovery room at Accident and Emergency, where I'd also given the nurse the empty tablet bottles so that they knew which tablets she had taken.

Mary had apparently been ditched by her first boyfriend, hence the photograph of him in her hand. The hospital had pumped out her stomach contents and according to the doctor her survival would be touch and go. There was nothing more that I could have done and the pressure was now off, so Sadie and I went outside for a fag, which I had difficulty in lighting because I was shaking so much. The doctor had been quite categorical about the fact that the prompt first aid had probably saved her life; and when I phoned the day after I was told that Mary would be okay. That was music to my ears and it left me with an odd sort of feeling that I can't explain. The incident had taken place in an area of the city that I didn't normally work in; and due to the fact that I didn't want to embarrass her I had never seen her since that day.

If I'd attended the incident in this day and age that critical ten minutes would have been lost. I wouldn't have dared to slap Sadie into action and certainly wouldn't have dared to touch a naked young lady. As far as Sadie and I were concerned there was no other options. The people who always know best what to do are never there when it matters, and Sadie and I did what we thought was right and let common sense prevail.

At the time, when I'd gone outside the hospital for a fag, I was shaking from head to foot because of the adrenalin rush brought on by the need for urgent action. For a few years after that it concerned me that I had shaken so much until one day I talked to a doctor friend about it who explained to me that it was caused by the body's natural reaction when placed in such a situation. This is crazy I thought, I'm shaking as much now as I was then. The thoughts of meeting her, knowing that she wanted me to attend for some reason, made me feel uneasy and I was dreading it. What would I say to her? What would she say to me? I knew it would be a very emotional time. I'd never been in a situation like this before and I lit another fag.

Although both Christine and I had been invited to the party, we had decided that I would go alone because Christine was heavily pregnant at the time.

After tea, I put on my new suit (which I'd stupidly forgotten to pick up from Mr Dar's a couple of weeks previously), combed my hair, straightened my tie and put my fags and matches in my pocket and I was ready for off.

My mate Alec arrived to pick me up and Christine kissed me cheerio telling me at the same time to just go and enjoy it. The party was at the Whitley Hall hotel at Ecclesfield and after Alec had dropped me off I stood outside for ten minutes; and with my hand shaking I lit up another fag. I was a big strong lad and had had many a scrap but the thoughts of this meeting were more frightening to me than any scrap I'd ever been involved in.

Right pal, I said to myself, in we go, let's do it. I took a deep breath and headed into the hotel; and I thought it was quite ironic that the tune I heard coming from the large room was the Beatles' *It's been a Hard Day's Night*. There must have been about a hundred people of varying ages inside, some singing and dancing and others just standing and talking. I couldn't wait to get to the bar for a pint. That's better I thought as I grabbed the pint and knocked it back fairly quickly. It calmed me down a bit as I looked round the room and tried to spot Sadie. It wasn't surprising that I couldn't spot her because when we first met we weren't exactly talking face to face and I couldn't remember what she looked like. The same applied to young Mary as I looked round for her. The last time I'd seen her was when I was holding her up from behind so I didn't see her face much and it didn't help that she was unconscious at the time.

By the same token Sadie obviously wouldn't recognize me either, but knowing that she was expecting me I started to look for a middle-aged lady who might keep looking around her. I still couldn't spot her so I asked the manager of the hotel if he could point out the lady who had organized the party. He kindly pointed her out and I walked over towards her. She looked totally different to the last time I had seen her which, under the circumstances of that day, was understandable. She was chattering away and smiling and the smile got bigger when I explained to her who I was; but I also saw a tear in her eye just as there was in mine. I can assure you that it was an emotional moment. I took Sadie to the bar and away from the crowds and asked her to point out Mary for me. Dancing away with the rest of them was a beautiful young woman who looked as if she hadn't got a care in the world. I would never have recognized her in a million years.

Sadie was really excited that I was there and explained to me that no one knew that I was coming but also and more importantly to me was the fact that Mary had never made a secret of her suicide attempt; and all the people at the party were aware of it. She was only young and very naïve at the time, and Sadie went on to say that she was now happy and had a new long-standing boyfriend; and her life was back on track. Apparently, ever since Mary had left the hospital she had wanted to meet me to say thank you and knowing that her 21st birthday wasn't far away Sadie had decided to try and find me as a surprise for Mary. At this point Sadie went back to her friends and I went back to the bar and stood watching people enjoying themselves on this happy occasion.

About fifteen minutes later and at the end of one of the dances Sadie shouted for everyone to be quiet for a few moments and also grabbed hold of Mary's hand. She gave a speech about Mary's life and the fact that her father had died when she was a young girl and she also mentioned the little blip that she had had about five years ago and the fact that as a mother she was very proud of her daughter. She also spoke about her being a teacher and then went on to say, 'We have a special surprise for you tonight, Mary – someone you have wanted to meet for a very long time is here to say hello.'

From the comment that Sadie had made and from the startled look on Mary's face I knew that she had twigged who the surprise guest was, and as I slowly walked towards her on the dance floor you could have heard a pin drop. Thank goodness I'd had a few beers to calm me down. At that point Mary ran towards me with tears running down her cheeks and I'm not embarrassed to say that I was also crying. What a moment! We gave each other a hug and everybody applauded. She introduced me to her new boyfriend; and if she blurted out 'thank you' once she must have said it a hundred times. We sat for ten minutes and she held my hand as we chatted away.

At that point the music kicked off again and she and her boyfriend went on to the dance floor. It was magical; and one of the most satisfying moments of my life when I saw her laughing, smiling, bright-eyed and happy. I could see that once more Mary was full of life which, for obvious reasons, made me very happy as well and for some reason I also felt very humble.

I've never been much good at dancing but I'd no choice when Sadie grabbed me and pulled me onto the dance floor. To my surprise everybody applauded and I felt a bit of a twerp but I also have to say that I felt very proud to be there that night. After that I went back to the bar and chatted with lots of different people and I can't remember paying for a pint all night; having said that I got a taxi home but I can't remember much about that either. It turned out to be one of the happiest days of my life.

A policeman's life can take many guises and we can sometimes be ridiculed for things that go wrong. We can only do and try our best when quick decisions need to be taken. Occasionally as humans we can get things wrong but fortunately on this occasion everything turned out for the good.

Unfortunately Sadie passed away a few years ago and Mary and her partner moved to somewhere in Scotland to work as a teacher.

CHAPTER 6

A Calculated Risk

'What time is it – what's up?' I yelled downstairs to Christine.

'11am and we're due at mum's at 12.30 for dinner, come on get up,' she replied.

'What day is it?'

'Sunday, that's why we're going to mum's.'

My head was pounding as I slowly climbed out of bed. Bloody hell, why do I feel like this, I thought, and then I suddenly remembered the night before with Mary and Sadie.

'Come on hurry up!' Christine shouted again. 'I've filled you a cold bath – that'll make you feel better.'

She was right, after a luke-warm bath I did feel better and I went down stairs and had toast and strawberry jam, lovely.

Three hours later and after eating a cracking Sunday dinner at Christine's mum's I was okay again; apart from the lousy weather, it was chucking it down with rain.

Christine and her mum were watching some programme or other on BBC TV so I decided to go and have a swift pint and a game of snooker with my mate, an older policeman called Les Igoe, who lived in a police house at the top of Oliver's Mount; and only a few yards away from the massive Brown Bailey's Sports Complex, which was one of the best in the country at that time. You name it – they'd got it: football pitches, cricket pitches, hockey squares, netball areas, running track, tennis courts, crown green bowling greens and cricket nets; and all provided by the giant steel manufacturing company for the benefit of their employees and families – how benevolent, great.

A large two-storey building contained sports equipment downstairs, and upstairs was the bar area which contained, amongst other things, a lovely old snooker table. From the front window you had magnificent views over a large part of Sheffield, but on this day all you could see were clouds and heavy rain.

Les and I got to the top of the stairs and Ron the steward turned to his wife Margaret, saying 'Didn't we bar these two barmy buggers a few weeks ago?' and laughed. Margaret also laughed and said, 'Nay Ron don't say that, we've no customers just now. The football teams have finished playing and gone and everybody else has gone home for their Sunday dinners.'

I'd known Margaret and Ron for several years and they always welcomed the police into the club. For some reason Ron never called me by my first name; instead he always called me 'Barnsley'.

Les and I had won a frame each and so we decided to play the best of three – neither of us were very good at snooker, but it just made a change and we were both enjoying it. Before starting the third game I decided to go downstairs to the gent's toilet, which was outside – I'd have to run like mad or I'd be like a drowned rat. Ron must have realized what I was doing and shouted downstairs, 'Barnsley, don't go out in the rain, use the ladies, everybody's gone home and the toilets aren't locked.' The ladies toilets were inside the building, which would save me getting wet through.

'Don't much fancy that Ron, but if you say so I'll do just that'; and off I went into the ladies loo. Like the gents it had showers but no urinals. Off I went into one of the two cubicles. Great, someone had left an old newspaper in there so I grabbed it and sat there reading.

A few minutes later I thought I could hear women's voices. This can't be right, I thought, Ron told me that there was no one here and knowing where I was, if someone had turned up he would surely have come and told me – or would he? I froze and as I listened, the talking got louder, the outside door opened and I heard footsteps going into the cubicle at the side of where I was sitting – this is crazy I thought to myself – what am I going to do?

The talking got louder and louder and I could tell from the conversation that the girls were undressing and taking a shower after complaining about the rain and mud. At the same time I heard the toilet flush in the cubicle next to me – I was like a rat in a trap and I just didn't know what to do. Talk about panic – I was terrified of being seen in such circumstances. I could see the headlines in the *Sheffield Star* newspaper: 'Pervert PC found in Ladies' Toilets'.

I'd locked the door when I first heard the voices and now I was sweating like a stuck pig. I was living a nightmare and I suddenly realized that someone might see my feet under the cubicle door so I lifted them up and 'spragged' them against the door as I sat there. All I could hear was singing and swearing and then I heard the word 'hockey' and realized then who the girls were. I hadn't got a clue how many players were in a hockey team but it sounded to me, in my predicament, that there were dozens of them.

The flush kept going in the toilet next door – hell fire, what if they run out of toilet paper, I thought and I was in two minds about throwing the newspaper over the dividing wall, at least it would be better than nothing. My heart was beating twenty to the dozen and it felt like it was going to jump out of my chest. It seemed as though I'd been sitting there for hours, hardly daring to breathe.

After about twenty minutes the noise started to subside – thank goodness for that I thought but I still dare not move a muscle, even though my legs were cramping up. After a further few minutes of agony I decided that the girls had gone, so I lowered my feet and tried to stand up but my legs wouldn't support me and I had to sit back down for a few minutes until the circulation came back. My ordeal was now over so I unlocked the door and walked out of the cubicle just at the same time as a woman burst back in through the outer door. It was absolutely bizarre, she looked at me in amazement with the weirdest look on her face and she said, 'I've left my hockey bag behind.' For once I could hardly open my mouth to speak but simply blurted out that I was the toilet cleaner, at which stage she nodded, grabbed her bag and fled.

Back upstairs, Ron and Margaret got the shock of their lives when they saw me, the bar shutters were down and they were just locking up to leave the club.

'Les's wife, Joyce, came to fetch him for his dinner and I thought you must have gone with him,' said Margaret, 'where have you been all this time?' And she looked at me in shocked amazement. When I explained my predicament they were both hysterical at the thought of it all.

'Bloody hell,' said Ron. 'I'd forgotten that there was a hockey match on, you can't see them from up here and their cars must have been parked on the other side of the ground. Sorry Barnsley.' He was still laughing his head off when he locked up the club and we all left together and as the three of us were leaving I shouted back to Ron, 'Don't forget to clean the toilets, there's mud everywhere and no toilet rolls,' and he gave me a quizzical look.

During the past few weeks we'd had several spates of burglaries at commercial premises in and around Fir Vale, Page Hall, Firth Park and Grimesthorpe but the main concentration was on Petre Street (why they spelled it like that I've no idea, I think the town planners must have had a few too many, everybody who knows the street pronounces it Peter even though it is spelt as Petre). Some of the burglaries had taken place just outside our police division and nearer to the city. The big boss was going loopy and he decided that enough was enough and he demanded action.

In those days burglar alarms were far less sophisticated than they are today and in a lot of cases the alarm systems had been tampered with; and thus prevented the alarm from activating when the building was entered, certainly a first for me and all the other lads I spoke to; so whoever was doing the jobs must have been very clued up. The other odd thing about it were the items that were stolen.

When visiting a crime scene the nature of the items that had been stolen will often give you a clue as to who may have committed the burglary and also the likeliest places to look in the hope of its recovery. If a burglar had a ready market for what he was stealing then that is what he would specialize in because he would have a ready outlet for the items. Conversely, sometimes what the perpetrator had left behind could be an indication that they hadn't got a market for such things and therefore we would have an idea of who not to look for. Over a period of time you got to know local criminals and their habits; and you knew what they would steal; it became part of their modus operandi.

In most of the burglaries that we were looking at, the items stolen ranged from calculators (whatever they were), pens, notepads, staplers, sticky tape dispensers and petty cash. It was weird. The methods of entry into the buildings were often made by breaking a window and lifting up the transom window catch thus giving access to the property. Some of the buildings that had been broken into had glass panels in the doors, what a delight for the burglar. All he had to do was stand with his back to the door, wait until no one was looking, take off his jacket and hold it behind his legs. At that point the glass panel could be given a backward kick and the sound of breaking glass would be muffled by the jacket. Whoever was doing the burglaries knew just what they were doing.

Over a period of several weeks officers from both the city division and ourselves watched certain areas from different positions, some on foot and some in cars – it was like trying to find a needle in a haystack. Where would they strike next?

One Sunday evening Rick and I were keeping observations in an unmarked police car on Petre Street, which at that time was fairly devoid of houses but yet full of small factory-type buildings. We both lit up; this was going to be a long night. We'd brought a flask, sandwiches and a couple of bananas along with a pack of cards and a torch apiece.

At roughly 7pm, and through the darkness, we spotted two lads of about fourteen years of age ambling towards us, which gave us no cause for concern. We were parked up and hidden in the car park of Mudfords who were world famous for making tents and marquees. As the lads went past us on the other side of the road, you could see that they were chattering away with not a care in the world, just as you and I would have been at that age. A few minutes later they reappeared and once more they walked past us in the direction of the city. As we were watching them disappear they suddenly stopped walking, turned and looked from side to side. What were the kids doing I wondered? At that point they walked down the entrance path leading to a company that, as far as I can remember, manufactured curtains.

'What's them two laiking about at Rick?' I said.

'What's laiking mean, pillock?' Rick said laughingly.

'It's a Barnsley expression for playing,' I explained. 'Come on lets go and see what they're up to.'

We left the car and luckily for us there was a high perimeter wall surrounding the car park at Mudfords. We hid behind it where we could observe the lads to see what they were up to. They were standing by a side door leading into the building which was lit by a small security light above the door. Then unbelievably one of them climbed onto the shoulders of the other and you could see him messing about with the alarm box which was fastened to the wall.

'Bleeding hell,' said Rick. 'It looks as though we're in here mate. Radio to tell the others.'

We knew that there were several cars and a police dog and handler watching the area just as we were. All were within a mile of us, so I radioed them to stay where they were until further notice. I also asked the police dog handler to get as near to us as he could without being seen and await further instructions just in case the lads did a runner.

Two or three minutes later the lad who had been on the shoulders of the other climbed back down. They both then took off their jackets and while one held both jackets in front of the bottom pane of glass in the door, the other one swung his foot and we could hear the muffled sound of breaking glass. At that point it was an attempted burglary so we waited until both lads entered the building thinking that they would be in there for, maybe, five or ten minutes.

Rick and I slowly crossed the road towards them in the hope that we were going to catch them red handed but just as we got to the other side of the road we saw them both climb back out of the door; and at the same time they saw us and started to run. They had been in the premises for less than two minutes, we couldn't believe it. Rick and I gave chase as they ran towards the city. We were just managing to keep pace with them for the first fifty yards or so when two things happened at once.

The lads had turned right and were running up the path towards the Hall Car Tavern, with us in pursuit and at the same time I heard someone shout, 'I've let the dog off.' I turned to see that the dog handler's van was parked just behind us and he had obviously answered our call to assist. At the same time I could see the dog bounding up towards us.

'What a bloody idiot. How is the dog to know that we are police?' I shouted to Rick as we both froze to the spot. If we'd moved a muscle the dog would have been on to us and having been in a similar position before when I was dragged around by a police dog at St Joseph's School (see *What's Tha Up To This Time?*). I didn't want another basin-full of that, so I stood still.

By now of course, the two lads had gone and instead of the culprits that we were after being chased by the dog it was us that had been caught instead! The dog handler rushed up to us and got the dog back on its lead; and Rick was going absolutely crackers about it.

Both Rick and I were puffing and panting after pursuing the lads and when I got my breath back I radioed to the other cars in the vicinity giving a rough description of the two young lads concerned; and also a rough estimation as to where they may be heading, while Rick proceeded to tear into the dozy police dog handler.

As we walked back to the burgled building we were both cursing like good 'uns. All that work for nothing and by so many people, what a ball-acher. The owner of the premises was sent for and on his arrival he told us that he couldn't see whether anything was missing or not; and that the alarm had, in fact, been messed about with.

Rick and I were amazed by it all. All within five minutes, they had disabled the alarm, broken into the premises and for what purpose? At this point we didn't know.

The following morning the receptionist arrived at work only to discover that her brand new hand-held calculator had been stolen together with some other small office equipment and petty cash to the value of about £12.

Rick and I at that time had never even heard of a hand-held calculator let alone ever seen one, apparently they had only recently been produced in America. The cost of one was about £170 – a lot of money in those days – and some of the first people to buy them owned small businesses as they saved them so much time and, as we all now know, they proved to be invaluable.

Luckily, the lads had been seen running in the Abbeyfield Road area and the city officers had managed to chase and arrest them near the Tea Gardens public house in Ellesmere Road. The young lads were in possession of the calculator but like us, the two officers didn't at first know what it was and had to be told. The young lads had readily admitted to committing that offence and quite a few others over the last few weeks. It turned out that one of them attended a private school and was extremely talented in engineering and electrical skills. At first they had started to disable the alarms and break into premises just for a laugh and to prove it could be done without setting off the burglar alarm.

At some point, and realizing what it was, they stole their first calculator. They showed it to the other lads at school and of course they all wanted one of these 'new-fangled' fancy gadgets. So the two Boy Wonders realized that they could make a nice little earner out of this if they sold them for a tenner a piece (vastly undervalued); and so they went on a mission to find and steal them. Being bright lads they worked out which sort of company would be likely to have them on the premises and then stole to order, just like professionals.

The arrest was dealt with by the city lads and Rick and I gave statements as to what we'd seen. It cleared up quite a lot of crime both for us and the city division. What the lad's parents must have thought I do not know but I would imagine that the lad with the brains probably now works in Silicon Valley in America – maybe one of the first of the 'brain drain' people to have left Britain.

Their calculated risk didn't pay off in the end and when you think that today we all use calculators on a daily basis it's hard to remember life without them.

CHAPTER 7

Some You Win and Some You Lose

The distance between Sheffield and Darfield, near Barnsley where I was born, was only about twelve miles, but our dialects were very different. When I first arrived in Sheffield in 1962 people couldn't understand half of what I was saying and conversely half of what was said to me I couldn't understand either. At times it could be very confusing. For example if someone in Sheffield told me that I was a 'bonny lad' I was dead chuffed as where I came from it meant attractive or nice looking. It came as a bit of a blow to me when I later found out that in Sheffield it meant someone who had a big and heavy build or was fat.

Another word widely used in Barnsley, but not in Sheffield, is the word 'laiking'. This word means playing or acting about. To confuse the matter even further if someone asked me 'a tha laiking' today? It could have two different connotations:

1. Are you playing out today?
or 2. Are you off work today?

I love fish cakes, but when I asked for one in a fish and chip shop in Sheffield I ended up getting two slices of potato with fish in between, deep fried in batter. That's what I called a scallop, and to me a fish cake was fish and mashed potato mixed with parsley and cooked in bread crumbs but this in Sheffield is called a 'rissole', something I'd not heard of before. I was probably one of the first Barnsley missionaries to Sheffield.

Some old Sheffielders say 'nar den dee' where as I would say 'nah then thee'; both are asking the same question, roughly interpreted as, 'hello how are you?'

I well remember a posh teacher from down south who was struggling to understand the dialect and he asked the question in class, 'Does anybody in this class know the Queen's English?'

'Yes sir I do,' I proudly replied, 'and I also know where she lives, sir – Buckingham Palace, in London.' For some reason the teacher must not have been happy with my reply as I had to stay in detention after school and write out one hundred times, 'I must learn to speak properly'. I didn't know what I'd done wrong but lines were better than the cane which I usually got.

I can honestly say that I hated school and I would wag it as often as I could, especially at exam times, no wonder that I never passed any.

Apart from school, all my memories of growing up in Darfield were happy ones. The only rules in our house were:

1. Always respect your elders.
2. Be polite, kind and generous towards other people.
3. Be honest with other people as well as yourself and
4. Listen – rather than speak. I'm not sure what happened to the last rule because these days I never shut up talking and could send a glass eye to sleep.

I loved Sheffield people and especially the ones in the division where I worked, the east end or 'rough end'. Like the coal miners in the Barnsley area, they were grafters and 90 per cent of them worked in the steel and steel-related industry and, like us Barnsley folk, called a spade a spade. I cannot stand pretentious people who think they are better than anyone else; and I've never been impressed by people who try to impress me. Indeed, the opposite applies; and I always try to look after the underdog.

A regular saying in Sheffield that I used to hear was, 'that bloke's that heavy he'd need Tommy Ward's crane to pick him up or his elephant to drag him'. When I asked why it was said and what it was about, no one seemed to know.

Being the major steel capital of the world meant that a lot of different types of metal that had been stolen from different places in the UK ended up in Sheffield through various illegal routes. It was such a major problem that as a police force it was decided to form the Stolen Metal Squad, the members of which specialized in just that – the investigation of stolen metal.

One day John and I were told to go to the gaffer's office where he would give us some instructions. So off we went. Apparently one of the members of the Stolen Metal Squad had received a tip-off that the premises of Tommy Ward's scrap business was going to be broken into and the safe was going to be blown. The boss told us that tomorrow we needed to bring enough food with us to work to last us for maybe twelve hours as we were going to stake out the building. Stake outs were all right provided something happened, but if nothing happened, which was often the case, they could become very, very boring – a word that I would normally never use. It was all part of the job and we all had to do it from time to time. It also presented a problem because Tommy Ward's huge head office was in Saville Street in Sheffield, near the city centre, but the other office, which was also large, was in our division on Attercliffe Common; and roughly opposite the old tram sheds at the top of Weeden Street, Tinsley.

The informant, whoever he was, had not said which of the offices were going to be broken into so that meant that both buildings had to be covered as they both contained safes.

We all assumed that the chosen offices to be screwed would be the main one in the city and for that reason more officers were deployed within that building, as well as conveniently-placed officers outside and in the immediate area.

At about 7pm when the office staff had gone home and all was quiet, John and I, along with two uniformed lads who, like us, were now dressed in jeans and jumpers, were spirited into the Tinsley offices, by the office manager. We also knew that there were officers strategically placed in unmarked cars in the vicinity, should we require assistance.

Between the two premises there were a lot of officers involved which, to us, was a good sign that the powers that be were satisfied with the information that they'd been given and we also knew that the safe blower himself was one of the top men in his profession. Let's hope that he breaks into our premises and not the other one, thought John and I – it would make a change from stolen pedal cycles, thefts from cars and house break-ins.

During all my working years in Attercliffe all of us lads had dealt with varying incidents where mainly kids would climb over the walls into the huge scrapyard and 'borrow' different items which they would often take to school and play with. Unbelievably, some of these 'borrowed' items included hand grenades, mortar bombs and such like which had all arrived at the yard after the Second World War; and even today live shells are still being recovered from various parts of the city.

At Attercliffe police station there was a specially made brick compound built in the yard which was filled with sand bags. This was to house the various items of munitions until they could be collected and destroyed by the bomb disposal unit, based at Strensall Army Barracks in York. Tommy Wards was, undoubtedly, the biggest scrap business in Sheffield that recycled old munitions recovered from military basis all over the country.

First things first. On entering the building we found the 'snap room' or canteen and mashed a pot of tea whilst there was still daylight. The flasks could be used later on during the night.

As I grabbed my pot of tea and walked into the reception area, I nearly dropped, bow legged. There on the wall were several pictures showing, of all things, an elephant in a harness pulling a large four-wheeled flatbed cart with heavy machinery on top of it. I was absolutely amazed. Also on the wall was the written history of Tommy Ward's which I found fascinating as I read it. It's a long time ago now but as far as I can remember Tommy Ward was born in the Victorian era and left school at the age of fifteen. He went on to become a very well-known and respected scrap dealer. He must have been a very 'with it' guy with an amazing 'nose for a deal' because over the years he went on to own breakers yards in several ports around Britain and, unbelievably, he broke up obsolete war ships and also luxury liners. One of the vessels that he broke up was a White Star liner which was towed to his breakers yard somewhere near Morecambe. The information went on to say that the White Star liner had previously been commanded by Captain Smith, who famously went down with his new ship the *Titanic*, after it hit an iceberg in 1912.

Mr Ward must have been an incredible business man and in 1913, I think it was, he was honoured with the prestigious office of Master Cutler, in Sheffield; but why the elephant? I couldn't understand it until I read further. It would appear that Tommy Ward's as a business was at its height in the First World War and because of the shortage of horses which were required on the Front Line, the indomitable Mr Ward didn't stick fast; and incredibly found an elephant called Lizzie which he leased in order to pull his carts around Sheffield, instead of the horses. He also hired a man to look after her and Lizzie became an everyday sight in Sheffield, hauling steel and machinery from place to place – how amazing is that? I couldn't stop laughing and realized that not far from the offices we were in, we used to work traffic duty twice a day. The thoughts of me working traffic and putting my hand up in order to stop an elephant which was lumbering towards me had me in stitches – what a sight that must have been.

I don't know what happened to Mr Ward and I don't think the company exists any longer but, Mr Ward, I take my hat off to you, what an entrepreneur!

Before placing ourselves in strategic parts of the building where we had good vantage points, I told the lads about Lizzie and Mr Ward but they weren't in the least bit interested. I couldn't believe it – the miserable farts.

For some reason when I look back, I realized that most of the stake-outs had taken place in the winter when it's dark for longer and also colder. Sods law being what it is tonight was such a night, dark and cold. For obvious reasons we couldn't have the lights on in the premises and I assumed that the heating must be going off as it was getting colder by the minute. I positioned myself where I could see the safe. John was near the main entrance and the other two lads were in their own positions overlooking the yard. We were all togged up with warm clothing and we had a very small torch for emergency use only. John had the only radio which was only to be switched on and used if we came under attack. There were no mobile phones in those days.

Sitting in the dark in a virtually empty building might sound easy to you but I can assure you that it isn't. After a while your eyes get used to the dark and it's amazing what you can actually see; but the main problem is noise. Every little noise that you hear puts you on high alert. It could be something or nothing at all. When you keep looking at your watch you look at it again in the hope that you've got it wrong. Ten minutes can seem like an hour and an hour can seem like four hours.

As the cold started to bite I decided that I would have a couple of swigs of tea on the hour and every hour and hoped that that would last me. Although I couldn't see them I could often hear the scampering of a mouse, at least I hoped it was a mouse and not a rat. At least I could see part of the yard and a bit of the main Attercliffe Road from two different windows; and I kept moving very stealthily from one to the other.

One hour, two hours, three hours went past and I decided to eat my chicken sandwiches just for something to do. When it got to 11 o'clock there was only the odd car or two passing the building and I knew that I had to be on my toes because I'd assumed that if there was going to be an attempt to break in it would more than likely take place between 2am and 4am when all sensible people would be snoring their little heads off in order to be ready for work the following morning. Every time I heard a dog bark or any other noise for that matter my senses kicked in and I was like a coiled spring. I assumed that the other lads were in the same state as I was and hoped they weren't asleep.

I kept thinking about Mr Ward and how he'd built his business up to what it is, and from the age of fifteen – amazing. Some, but not all of the scrap lads were likely lads handling stolen property and I wondered whether he himself had started up that way. Common sense told me that he wouldn't have been given the prestigious title of Master Cutler if he'd been a rogue or had a criminal past. It was people like him who had worked hard and helped to make Sheffield the city that it is today.

I finished my last sip of tea at about 5 o'clock in the morning and reasoned that the optimum time for breaking into the premises had gone. We also knew that we would have to vacate the premises before 7am when the cleaners and workforce would start to arrive. By 6 o'clock I could see that one or two cars were using the main road and I polished off my last sandwich and banana. I'd had enough and could have murdered a pint, so I tiptoed down to reception where jammy John had found a comfortable chair; but to his credit he was wide awake. I went to find the other lads who were also both wide awake and just like John and me totally knackered and fed up. It was obvious that nothing was going to happen that night at least, so John switched on the radio and spoke to control.

All the fun and games must have taken place at Tommy Wards head offices in Saville Street but when John got on the radio he was told that it was the same there, nothing had happened and all officers deployed on both stake outs were told to stand down. What a waste of time! I had to chuckle at the thought of twenty to thirty officers all cursing at the same time when they heard the news.

We left the premises at 6.30am and all four of us were gagging for a pint, we were as dry as old bones; and if we went home at this unearthly hour we would all wake up our respective families (that was our excuse anyway).

About a mile from where we were and on the same long road stood the Temple public house situated on the Sheffield/ Rotherham border, where Magna, the industrial museum, now stands. The pub was unusual because of its geographical location. It sat in the middle of the giant steel smelting furnaces then part of the British Steel Corporation. The night shift finished at 6am when the day shift would take over. The night shift workers had been working all night in the tremendous heat given off in the steel smelting process and for that reason the pub had a special licence to open at 6am to allow the steelworkers to replenish the liquids that they had lost while working – how opportune for us – and the four of us were in like a flash.

You could hardly move in the pub, there were loads of men young and old wearing flat caps with their white sweat towels tucked into their waistcoats, some of them were wearing clogs; and we stood out like sore thumbs as we ordered a pint a piece. I couldn't wait.

I was just about to take my first swig when John nudged me and whispered, 'F-----g hell. Look over there at those two blokes stood by the pillar.'

As I looked across I recognized a detective from Rotherham talking to another chap that I didn't know and at the same time the detective saw us and he and the other bloke disappeared.

'That's weird John,' I said, 'what's he doing in here at this time in a morning?'

John looked very serious indeed and he was silent for a few seconds before he said, 'Somethings not right here Martyn, did you know the other bloke?'

'No,' I said.

'Get this,' said John, 'it's only 'Bill Blogs' who was tipped to be blowing the safe tonight in Tommy Ward's.' When John said that my first mouth full of beer shot out of my mouth and I looked at him in amazement. Alarm bells were ringing in both our heads – what's going on? The pub didn't open until 6am and it was pure coincidence that we ended up there. John and the other lads had never been in before and I'd only been in once before, surely you wouldn't arrange to meet someone in a pub at that time in the morning – had they been out all night together?

After two pints we all went home and John was later asked for a report by one of the big bosses in CID. Unfortunately we never got to the bottom of what happened – or more importantly didn't happen that night but a few months later the detective we'd seen in the Temple pub left the force. There was obviously something very, very strange happening that night but us poor minions were never told anything about it. But it's something that I never forgot.

CHAPTER 8

A Grim Discovery

Bright-eyed and bushy-tailed, I arrived at Attercliffe police station at 8.30am. It was an absolutely glorious day; and when the schools were closed for their six weeks holiday, which they now were, the difference in time it had taken for me to get to work because of the lack of traffic was amazing. It was the end of the two weeks annual works shut down too, and thousands of people would have gone away for a week or two weeks break from their daily grind. Caravan sites on the east coast would be full and everyone would be enjoying themselves.

Unfortunately, as happened every year, some of these people would have returned to their homes only to find that they had been broken in to; people had saved up all year round to afford a simple holiday with their families only to return to the trauma of finding out that their houses had been burgled by some mindless moronic 'pillock'.

As I walked up the stairs I anticipated a busy day, so I put the large kettle on the gas stove ready for the arrival of Rick and John. By the time they arrived there were three steaming hot pint pots of tea on the table, along with three Kit Kat bars which I'd bought at the shop.

'Service with a smile,' said John as he grabbed his tea, 'just what we want today, thanks.'

As people had arrived home from their holidays on either a Saturday night or Sunday night and found their houses burgled, a short report would have been taken by the uniformed lads leaving us to take statements and investigate the crime.

Historically, people who lived in the posher areas of the city with their fancy houses would contact the police telling them that they were going to be away on holiday and could they please keep an eye on the house while they were gone. That had gone on for years but very few people in our division, where the working-class tended to live, did that, and therefore just left it to chance, getting away without telling anybody.

A problem arose when some of the people who had reported that they were going to be away bragged to other people, 'Oh, the police are going to look after our house while we're away.'

Inevitably, whenever people heard comments like that it prompted them to do the same, so it wasn't long before this became a problem as more and more people wanted their houses checking by the police in order to live up to the Joneses. Each householder that went on holiday gave their name and address to the police station; and whichever officer was working the beat in that vicinity was given a reference card with details of the house to be checked on it. Each house had to be visited once per shift or in other words, three times a day. After every visit we had to sign the card giving the time that we had visited and checked the property and these cards were checked by the duty sergeant or inspector.

Visiting between thirty and fifty houses and having to prove that you had done so in one 8-hour shift was one hell of a workload, and had to be done in between dealing with road accidents, thefts and domestic disputes – it was nigh on impossible. The whole idea was totally stupid and also counterproductive. What no one had taken into account was the fact that people in the better-off areas of the city had a minimal number of burglars living around them, whereas our division, being the rougher end of town, contained more burglars than any other part of the city. It soon became obvious to the local criminal fraternity that a policeman seen walking up the garden path to a particular house was a sure sign that those people were away. This stupid situation went on until it was realized that the majority of houses we were visiting were getting broken into, more than likely, after the last policeman's visit. The police, as usual, got the blame and the system was eventually stopped. There's nothing wrong with asking the police to keep an eye on your property whilst you are on holiday if it's done in a random manner but its far better to quietly mention that you are going away to a trusted neighbour.

Luckily, things had calmed down a bit by this time and between John, Rick and myself we had less burglaries to attend to than at the same time last year. At last common sense had prevailed and people were asking a neighbour to keep an eye on their houses instead of uniformed police.

We were more back to normal at this point and when Inspector Hepworth doled out a list of the current burglaries to look into

I was given four enquiries on the Manor estate and one enquiry on the nearby Woodthorpe Estate; whilst John and Rick were given eight enquiries to deal with, mainly in the Firth Park and Wincobank areas. For that reason John and Rick decided to work together and do the Wincobank side of the city whilst I took the Manor and Woodthorpe.

Pots of tea and Kit Kats were polished off and I grabbed a pile of statement forms and the key to one of the two Morris Minor unmarked cars at our disposal, and I was off. I made my way up the 'Cliffe' and then down Staniforth Road to Darnall where I turned right up Prince of Wales Road towards the infamous Manor estate.

Back in those days burglar alarms were only seen in the richer suburbs of the city and where I was going no one could afford one. The first three houses that I called at, which were all fairly close to each other, had all been broken into by sticking a large piece of brown paper on the rear window and near to the transom catch. A punch with a fist or a brick had caused the window to break and the splinters of glass, which were stuck to the thick brown paper, had then been removed and then discarded in the garden. The burglar had then put his hand through the window and reached up and released the catch and climbed in through the open window – a most unusual means of entry and one that I'd not come across before. Being fairly poor people there wasn't much to steal apart from a few trinkets and in one case a gold pocket watch.

I radioed in to ask the fingerprint lads to attend and drove about three-quarters of a mile away to a quieter part of the Manor; and on checking the door numbers as I was looking for the house that had been burgled I got a bit of a shock as I realized that I'd been to this house before some eight or nine years previously when I was in uniform.

As I pulled up near to the house I wound the windows down and lit up a fag; and as the memories of that day came flooding back I nearly lit up another; and almost had a fag in each hand. Thinking about the previous situation I found myself in when I last visited this house made me shudder. It had been a day very similar to today's in that it was red hot and I'd been working my beat on a push bike, in just shirt-sleeve order. At about 10am that day the postman who was carrying a large bag waved to me and asked me to stop. I wondered what he wanted, surely he couldn't have been lost on a job like he had. He looked very agitated, 'How can I help you mate?' I asked with a smile.

'I'm the regular postman in this area and I know almost everyone by their surnames,' he answered.

'Very good,' I said, 'I'll bet they know you as well.'

He pointed to a semi-detached house that was set back further from the road than some others and said that he was worried about Mr _____ who lived at that house.'

'Why are you worried about him?' I casually asked.

'I used to see him knocking about, usually when he's going to work but that was before they moved me to the postal route at Woodhouse. I didn't start back on this route until about three weeks ago and when I push his mail through the letter box it makes a sound as if it's dropping onto a pile of papers or letters and not the usual sound that it makes when it lands on the floor. So I don't think he's dealing with his mail.'

'Have you tried knocking on the door?' I asked.

'Yes several times but I don't get an answer.'

'Have you asked the people next door about him?'

'I can't do 'cos the man in the post office says that the lady next door has gone to visit her daughter in Australia for a year, so I can't ask her.' He looked really concerned and worried. 'I've been going to go to the police station for the last few days but I didn't want to appear to be a nosy parker so I'm glad I bumped into you now.'

'Right, let's go and have a look then,' I said.

Both houses were set back from the road and it looked as though it had once been a cul-de-sac but there were no houses on either side of the road. A loud knocking on the door produced nothing; and both front and back downstairs windows had got lace curtains up to them; but all the main curtains in the house were open. Looking through the lace curtains in the front window I couldn't see anything untoward, so I went to the letter box to see if I could see anything through that. As I did so the smell hit me in a big way – the stench of death – and I closed the letter box quickly, and started to gip. Making my way to the back of the house, I managed to find an old zinc wash tub which I stood on to look over the top of the lace curtains.

'Bloody hell fire!' The kitchen/dining area contained the usual square table, just at the right of which, was a chair. To the left was a two-bar electric heater, which was switched on. As I looked at the chair I could see the torso of a man clad in a white vest but I couldn't see his head. I scrunched up my eyes in order to see better into the room and got a shock as I could see, what I was pretty sure, was the man's head on the floor and a little way from the body.

The postman was looking at me when I jumped down off the tub so I broke the news to him and took his details, telling him that I might need to see him later; and thanked him very much for his public spiritedness, sending him on his way. We had no radios in those days and my mind was racing as I cycled to the nearest telephone box to ring the Duty Sergeant at the nick.

Even though there didn't appear to have been a forced entry into the house, it could still have been murder – how did his head end up on the floor? I'd been told to await the arrival of a detective inspector who later arrived along with a pathologist and a police photographer. They each stood on the zinc wash tub in turn to get a view through the window just as I had done, and on seeing what I had seen drew the same conclusion – murder – time to break into the house!

Not wanting to disturb a possible crime scene, it was decided to tie a rope, borrowed from somewhere or other, around my chest so that when I smashed open the front door I didn't end up in the house itself.

I hit the door with my shoulder and it gave way fairly easily, just enough to allow entry. When the door gave way everyone jumped back along with me, the stench was absolutely revolting and we were all just about throwing up in a big way, including the pathologist. The house was full of blue bottles, some of which were now flying out of the door, you cannot imagine in your most horrible nightmares just what the smell was like.

No one would enter the house, it was that bad, the stench, the maggots and the blue bottles were everywhere and so the detective inspector contacted, what I believed, was the ambulance service who brought out two special one-piece coveralls and breathing apparatus – it was that bad. Being the junior officer I was, thankfully, asked to wait outside whilst the detective inspector and police photographer slowly made their way into the stinking house. I certainly didn't envy them their job.

Apparently, photographs were taken during the very slow search of the house and on the kitchen table a shaving mug and a stick of shaving soap could be seen. The body was sitting opposite the kitchen sink which had a mirror above it and between that and the sink a cut throat razor, along with a shaving brush was found on the floor. There was also a haversack on the table containing a pack of rotted sandwiches and work gear.

During the next couple of hours there were lots of discussions and the pathologist concluded that the man must have got up early to get ready for work and during the process of shaving he must have coughed or sneezed and inadvertently slashed his jugular vein with the cut throat razor; and he also concluded that the heavy loss of blood made him weak so he must have stumbled back onto the chair in a collapsed state where he, unfortunately, died.

He also concluded that, because of the heat in the house, the body had decomposed very quickly and was attacked by blue bottles and flies. He estimated that death had taken place probably five to six months previously. The pathologist went on to say that the body was full of maggots which had fed on the deceased's internal organs and bodily fluids. When the body became skeletonized the head must had dropped forward breaking the spinal cord near the neck; and that was the reason that the head was separated from the body and on the floor.

I thought I'd got away with entering the house but as the police photographer and inspector removed their breathing masks and coveralls, the inspector then instructed me and a mortuary assistant to remove the body. The smell of the suits as they took them off was horrendous but now it was my turn to wear one along with the mask; and I was gipping already. The whole of the house floor was covered in the stinking mass of maggots and flies and I wished I'd gone down the pit to work with my dad instead of joining the force. As we lifted what was left of the body it more or less crumbled into a pile of bones and we then took him to the mortuary. An inquest was later held and it was recorded by the coroner as accidental death.

The Public Works department was sent for and as they were shovelling maggots up off the floor, we could now see the bloodstains obviously from the poor man as he bled to death. The house was boarded up.

Some of the not-so-near neighbours in the locality were asking questions as to what had happened – but amazingly none of them even knew the poor man.

I stunk like twenty middens and I later burnt my clothes including the uniform which the force replaced. It took me weeks before I felt clean again and I probably had more baths in two weeks than I had in two years; but I couldn't get the poor man out of my mind. To think that he'd been there dead all that time without anyone knowing. His workmates thought he'd must have taken early retirement so they weren't worried; what a shame they didn't take the trouble to find out for themselves. I wouldn't wish that day's events on any of you and even now some fifty years later I can still remember the sights and stench of that day; and it still makes me gip even thinking about it – how sad a day that was.

As I sat in the car thinking of that day I threw my second fag away. I could see two little toddlers playing in the front garden of the house which looked neat and tidy. I had a chat with the kids and knocked on the door, which, I'll be honest sent shivers down my spine. A young lady opened the door and broke down in tears when she realized who I was. I scanned the house which was spotlessly clean and tidy and I very, very much doubted if she knew of the circumstances of the man's death years previously – and I certainly wasn't about to tell her.

The job was the same as the others and, as a young family, they hadn't much to steal in the first place. Entry into the house had been made the same way as the others and I found a piece of thick brown paper still with slivers of glass stuck to it and discarded in the yard at the back of the house. They were a young family with very few material possessions and so after taking the statement and chatting with the kids over a pot of tea I left to go to the last job of the day. We all hated house burglars – as well as what they steal it's what they leave behind – trauma!

My next enquiry was about half a mile away and just as I arrived I could see that the whole of the large front window was smashed including the wooden centre support. The door was opened by Steve, one of the local likely lads who I'd helped out about a year before when three lads had got him down on the pavement as I was driving past. They were giving him a good kicking for whatever reason until I got out of the car and, on recognizing me, all three fled the scene. Like most of the likely lads Steve hadn't made an official complaint but said that he would sort it out in his own way. I chuckled to myself as I walked into the house and said, 'What's happened here Stevey boy? They've certainly not used brown paper covered in glue to break that window, have they?'

'The bastards – there must have been two of them. Look at this,' he said; and he pointed to a metal dustbin which had been filled with house bricks and then thrown through the front window; and he went on to say, 'It was about two o'clock this morning, look at damage it's done. Its smashed the television and china cabinet.'

'It looks as though you've upset someone Steve,' I said.

'Too right, Mr Johnson, and if I find out who's done it I'll upset the bastards even more.'

It was pointless sending for the fingerprints man here, I thought, so I took a statement, went back to the office and later home.

It might sound daft to you and you might think I'm a twerp, but as soon as I got home that evening I had a good long soak in the bath. Even after nine years the thoughts of the smell in that house still haunted me.

CHAPTER 9

The Dozy Pillock

A couple of days later saw me driving down the M1 to Nottingham. The weather had been gorgeous all week and it was a pleasure to be out. I arrived at Nottingham Police Headquarters and dropped little Sarah's case papers off in the police prosecutor's office. Mr Dirty Bastard was still in custody and awaiting trial later in the year, when it was anticipated that he would plead guilty, as charged.

I was done and dusted at 11am and earlier that morning Christine had sent me off to work with a bit of a treat for an old pal of ours, Les Jones, who lived at Inkersoll near Chesterfield, just off the M1 motorway. He was very partial to ginger biscuits, especially the ones we bought from the Rington's travelling salesman. I arrived at his house where he was doing some weeding in the garden.

'Come on Les, put that kettle on, I've been here thirty seconds already,' I shouted over the fence; and then added, 'I've brought you a packet of your favourite ginger biscuits to go with it.'

Les was a lovely man and originally from Shiregreen in Sheffield; and was very knowledgeable about the local area. We were both interested in local history and I'd learnt a lot from him over the years. The pot of tea and a few biscuits went down a treat, but work was calling and as I left Les said, 'Say hello to Christine and thanks for the biscuits.'

I was soon back on the M1 and heading back to what? You never knew what the day would bring on a job like ours. I'd forgotten to bring my snap that morning so I nipped into one of the local cafes near to the police station where I enjoyed a bacon, egg and tomato sandwich with Sarah who ran the café. She didn't look as happy as normal. The café was busy but she asked me if I could call in one morning when the café would be quiet as she needed a chat. I wondered what that was all about as I left the café; and went back to the nick to type up some reports. Boy did I hate typing, my bruised two finger ends felt like broken pit props.

I was just leaving to go home when the phone rang. It was Steve, the likely lad whose front window had been smashed in by someone throwing a dustbin full of house bricks through the window a few days before.

'Nah then Steve. How are things? I asked.

'All right, Mr Johnson – can I ask you a question?'

'Go on Steve. It depends what it is but I might be able to give you an answer. What's the problem?'

'You know the other day when you called at our house? When you saw our smashed window, did I hear you say that they'd certainly not used brown paper covered in glue to break that window,' Steve said.

'I can't remember Steve but I probably did because I'm looking into several burglaries where that method was used to break the window in order to gain entry into the house. Why do you ask?'

'I just wasn't sure whether I'd heard it right. That's all.'

'What shift are you on next week, Mr Johnson?'

'Afternoons, starting Monday at 3pm. Why?'

'Nothing, but I might give you a ring next week. Okay?' and with that he put the phone down.

I wondered what that was all about, but sometimes you're better off not asking and letting things take their course. He was obviously up to something but I put it to the back of my mind and went home. Anyway two days to go and it was my weekend off. I was really looking forward to it and if the weather stayed as it was, bright and sunny, I'd arranged with Rick to go haymaking at my sister's farm.

The weather kept its promise and the sun kept shining so I picked Rick up; and by 8.30am on the Saturday we were on our way to Lindley at the far side of Huddersfield, about twenty-five to thirty miles away. My brother-in-law John Beever was a hill farmer and he also had a fairly large milk delivery round where he dropped bottles of milk off at various houses in the surrounding area. Unfortunately he'd had a bit of a run in with a bull. It wasn't too serious but John had accidentally got himself trapped between the bull and the cowhouse door when something spooked the bull, which caused it to turn quickly, squashing John against the door, breaking him a few ribs; and he was in agony. The old saying is true: make hay while the sun shines; and John was stuck because of his injury with only himself and Alan Clough the farmer man to help him. So my sister Bronnie had phoned me to go and help. Even though Rick was a city lad, he'd been hay-making before on odd occasions and jumped at the chance of going with me. I was a fairly seasoned hand at the farm job and usually helped John or my uncle Jack most years.

I loved all the stone buildings and mills in Huddersfield, and as we drove up New Hey Road towards the M62 I couldn't wait, the scenery from the farmhouse was spectacular. At Outlane we turned right and drove past the oddest named pub that I'd ever come across, The Wappy Spring. Just past the pub we turned left, over the motorway and the farm, Haigh House Hill was on our left (I think the farm is now a small garden centre, but I'm not sure). As we drove into the farmyard I looked to my right and could see right across to Halifax, Greetland and Hebden Bridge; and wondered how several pals of mine were who lived there: Kath and Steve Beasley along with Brian Hargreaves who lived at Greetland.

John was already in the farmyard along with Alan who had also brought his dad Harold to help. Great, so that meant that there were four of us. That'll do nicely, I thought.

A few years prior to this the M62 had been built straight through the middle of John's farm, losing him lots of good grazing land and for this reason he'd had to rent Cop Riding Farm off an old chap called Joe Bairstow. After hitching up the trailers to the two Massey Ferguson tractors, we made our way to the very steep-sloping field in the bottom of the valley. How they worked on a hillside like that I don't know, but they'd been doing this for years. John had allowed Rick to drive one of the tractors, which he thought was a great novelty. Because the land was so steep we knew it was going to be hard going but, pitch forks in hand, off we went into the fields. It was bloody hard graft but worth it just to be out in the clean fresh air of the countryside made better by the knowledge that we were doing a good turn for John, who because of his injuries could only drive the other tractor. Harold, Alan's dad, wasn't a big man but he could do the work of ten men and between us both trailers were stacked high with bales of hay in what seemed like no time at all. We slowly headed back up the steep road to the farm. Rick had arrived back in the farmyard before us and I could see him standing next to the tractor with a puzzled look on his face.

'What's up?' I asked him.

'I think I'm going mad,' Rick answered with a puzzled expression on his face.

'Why? what have you done?'

'It's not what I've done it's what I've seen.'

'Are you going to tell me then or are you going to make me guess?'

'You'll never believe what I've seen, I couldn't believe my eyes.'

'Go on then tell me for goodness sake,' I said.

'I've just seen a yellow three-wheeler car.'

'Right, I've seen a few of them,' I replied.

'No – listen – this was a bit different, it had a coffin on the roof.'

'What!' I shouted.

'A coffin on top, but that's not all. There was a dog in the passenger seat with a crash helmet on its head.'

'I think you've had too much sun,' I said.

'No – honest, a bloke was driving a yellow three-wheeler car with a coffin on the roof and a dog was in the passenger seat with a crash helmet on its head'; and he cracked up laughing and so did I. We could hardly work for thinking about the crazy car.

When we had unloaded we headed back to the fields to carry on working. As we were passing the Wappy Spring pub, lo and behold, there parked in the car park was the yellow three-wheeler car. The coffin was still on the top and sitting on the top of that was the dog with the crash helmet on its head. We couldn't believe our eyes, and stopped to look.

'Hey, John. Come and look at this,' I shouted; and John came over. 'Look at that car in the car park.' He took a look and said, 'That's Mangle Worzel, he's a local man, and he's been driving that car like that for years. We were all doubled up with laughing – what a character. We did another stint in the afternoon and then helped John fill the milk bottles ready for his round the next morning. What a great day it had been – hard work, a good laugh and wonderful food that my sister had made for us.

When I got back to work on Monday afternoon I was as stiff as a board and my hands were as sore as hell from picking up the bails with the bailer twine and pitchforking them onto the top of the trailer; but it had all been well worth it, we'd got John out of a hole, eaten plenty of lovely snap and come home with some milk straight from the churn; and a tray full of fresh eggs – what could be better?

At about 4pm the phone rang in the CID office and Rick answered, 'DC Hardwick,' I heard him say, then he shouted across to me: 'Somebody called Steve wants a word wi' thi Martyn.'

'Is that you Mr Johnson?' said Steve.

'Heyup Steve, how can I help you this time?' I said.

'I'm working for a demolition company and I've just finished work; and I wondered if I could have a quick word with you. I'm only at Tinsley. Can I see you outside the police station in about ten minutes?' he asked in a hushed voice.

'No problem Steve, see you outside soon,' I answered.

As I stood outside the nick I lit a fag and I wondered what he wanted me for. He sounded a bit secretive, he's up to something, I thought to myself; and chuckled. A couple of minutes later a medium-sized lorry loaded with scrap pulled up alongside me but Steve, the driver, didn't get out but opened the window instead.

'One good turn deserves another, Mr Johnson. When you mentioned brown paper and glue used to break into them poor people's houses last week it wound me up. I hate bastards that do that, robbing their own kind. I don't do house burglaries, you know that Mr Johnson, I'm a metal man.'

'I know what you mean Steve,' and I chuckled because I'd pulled him a few times before for handling stolen metal. 'Right Steve, what's up lad, what can I do for you?' I asked.

'Nothing, it's my turn now – you helped me out when I was getting a good kicking and so I've done a bit of sniffing out for you. The burglar you're looking for wi' them jobs is called Mr Sticky Fingers (for want of his real name). This is his address'; and he passed me a piece of paper through the open window. As he started the engine on the lorry and started to drive away he shouted back: 'I don't think he'll do a runner once you've caught him'; and I heard him laughing as he drove off. What the hell is he on about, that's a funny thing to say I thought and shouted, 'Thanks Steve'; and he drove away. The name and address he'd given me meant nothing to me but when I showed it to Rick he knew of him.

'He's only small but a nasty little piece of work. His nick-name's Shorty but he certainly can fight. He used to do a bit of boxing. He's been locked up for violence in the past,' Rick explained.

Checking fingerprints in those days was far less advanced than it is today; and finding out who they belonged to without specific details was a long-winded process which had to be done manually and at this time of day the finger print department, as a whole, would now be closed. I'd have to wait until tomorrow to give them the suspects name to see if they could match his fingerprints against any of the prints (if any) left at the scene of the burglaries I was investigating.

Realizing that I couldn't get the prints checked until the next day put me in a bit of a dilemma. If I waited he could have committed another four or five burglaries and that was the last thing we wanted. I had a discussion with Rick and we decided to bring him in there and then before he had chance to do any more break-ins. In view of his violent past we also took with us a pair of handcuffs just in case.

We made our way up the Manor and got to the house concerned, which looked a right scruffy hole with dog muck all over the place. Luckily for us, as we walked down the garden path, the dogs were Labradors and friendly but filthy, poor things. Sitting in a deckchair in the back garden was Mr Sticky Fingers who immediately recognized Rick. Blimey he is small – Rick was right I thought, no wonder they called him Shorty.

He certainly didn't look like a burglar to me, he'd got a couple of plasters stuck to his face, a bandage round his head and his left arm and lower right leg were in plaster casts; and at the side of him were two crutches. Now I knew what Steve had meant when he said that he wouldn't do a runner when we caught up with him and inwardly I was laughing my little socks off; and wondered what had happened.

'You're under arrest Mr Sticky Fingers, for committing house burglaries on the Manor Estate,' I said; and cautioned him. 'What have you got to say about that?'

He shuffled in his chair nervously. 'Not me mate,' he said; and his bottom lip curled up in a snarl.

'Then how come your fingerprints have been found in different houses?' I asked; and his reply had me in stitches, what a dozy pillock.

'F-------- hell. I didn't think I'd left any,' he said. 'That's cos I was rushing.'

What an admission, you can't get better than that; and when I looked across at Rick he too was now openly laughing. It had to go down as one of the simplest interviews ever conducted.

'Where's the stuff that you've nicked Mr Sticky Fingers?' Rick asked.

'I've spent the money in the pub and the two gold watches are here'; and he fished them out of his pocket.

In the house he showed us a big roll of brown paper and a couple of tins of cow gum which we recovered for evidence. We didn't bother with the handcuffs because, as Steve said, he wasn't going to do a runner. As we set off to Attercliffe nick we bundled him into the front seat of the police car with difficulty and because of that I had to sit behind him; and I was rolling about with laughing thinking about his guilty reply. Just to make sure we'd got the right man we took a detour and he showed us the houses he'd burgled, including two in Woodseats Division that we were unaware of.

When we got into the police station we spoke to him in the waiting room to save him having to climb the stairs with his crutches and then Rick said, 'How have you got into that mess anyway?'

'I don't bleeding know,' he snarled. 'I went for a pint in the Fair Lea pub the other night and when I came out it was dark and something hit me at the back of the head and knocked me out I think.'

'But what about your leg and your arm?' Rick asked.

'When I came too I felt dizzy, some bastard had put me in a dustbin full of house bricks and rolled it down the hill with me in it until it hit a tree and stopped. I didn't know what was happening until somebody saw me and rung for an ambulance, that's how I broke mi leg and mi arm.'

My sides were splitting and I had to run out of the waiting room as I realized the implications with Steve's smashed window which Rick didn't know anything about. Tears were streaming down my cheeks at the thought of it all. He readily admitted to breaking into the houses plus a couple over the road in Woodseats Division, which is where the other gold watch had been stolen from; which we knew nothing about.

Apparently, Mr Sticky Fingers was overdue with his rent so had decided to burgle a few houses and when Rick took a statement off him he even complained, stating 'It's a waste o' time burgling houses round here they've nowt to nick. I only ended up with £10 and these two watches and I still owe for mi rent.' He was later charged and went on to plead guilty at court; and was sent to prison for, as far as I remember, nine months.

Oh and by the way, when I spoke to the fingerprint lads they'd only found two fingerprints, both of which were smudged to the degree that they wouldn't have been allowed as admissible evidence linking Mr Sticky Fingers to the jobs; so it was a good thing that he had coughed (admitted to the burglaries).

A couple of weeks later I bumped into Steve and thanked him and was laughing as I said, 'I think you've got your own back as well Steve,' but he didn't smile which I thought was odd.

'What's up?' I asked.

'I've dropped a bollock Mr Johnson – I'd been told that the lad who'd done your burglaries was also the lad who did my house with the dustbin – but I've since found out that it wasn't him who did my house, it was two lads from Woodthorpe who'd done it,' he said.

I know I was supposed to look serious about it but I just couldn't stop laughing; and I could see in my mind's eye Mr Sticky Fingers rolling down a hill in a dustbin and wondering what the hell was happening to him; and when I see an old metal dustbin on an allotment now it sets me off laughing again.

Things happen in funny ways but as far as we were concerned all's well that ends well and no one else will know any different (until now). As for Mr Sticky Fingers the burglar – he got his comeuppance.

CHAPTER 10

Little Chicago?

The first thing that hit me when I arrived in Sheffield in 1962, and especially in the 'East End' of the city where I worked, was the smoke, great clouds of it; and different colours making its way skywards. Sheffield had always and quite rightly been considered the steel capital of the world and, because of the river Don, water-driven forges were constructed. The city was famous for metal working hundreds of years before the Industrial Revolution, even as far back as medieval times.

After the Industrial Revolution, Sheffield expanded very quickly and during the First World War there were thousands of craftsmen employed in different capacities but mainly to do with the manufacture of munitions. Because of this, thousands of back-to-back, terraced houses with shared outside toilets were built in long rows, mainly in the central and eastern part of the city. The pollution was bad enough when I first arrived in the East End and I can't imagine what the amount of smoke would have looked like both during and in between the two world wars. No wonder George Orwell described Sheffield as the ugliest town in the world.

After the First World War businesses started to lapse slightly but in 1939 at the beginning of the Second World War Sheffield once more became a huge and thriving industrial city of about 500,000 inhabitants; which were policed by about 550 policemen and obviously amongst those 500,000 people there would have been quite a few villains.

Within a few months of me working the beat I would often hear people shouting at the children who were out playing, 'Get in this house now, it's nearly dark and Charlie Peace'll get you.' I hadn't a clue who Charlie Peace was and, because of the fact that I didn't know anyone in Sheffield and also had time on my hands after work, I took myself off to the library at the end of Worksop Road in Attercliffe, to find out.

Charles Frederick Peace was born in the slum area of Sheffield city centre in 1832. At some time or other in his younger life he must have gone to work in the steel works because, at the age of fourteen, he was permanently crippled in an accident at one of the rolling mills.

After quite a long time in hospital Charlie decided to embark on a life of crime and must have, at some time or other, ended up living in Manchester because in 1854 he was found guilty of a load of burglaries for which he was sentenced to four years in prison with hard labour. Upon his release in 1859 he married a widow, Hannah Ward. Soon afterwards he was caught committing a further major burglary in Manchester and almost killed the arresting police officer with a gun, for which he received a sentence of a further six years in prison, again with hard labour. You would have thought that this had taught Charlie Boy his lesson but yet again upon his release he was caught committing another burglary in Manchester, netting him another eight year stretch with hard labour. At that point he must have got absolutely fed up with Manchester and after his release from this sentence he moved back to his native Sheffield and lived in Darnall, where I later worked as a policeman.

Peace must have thought that everybody who lived in Manchester was rich because he next pops up in 1876 when at about midnight two policemen saw him entering the grounds of a large house, again in Manchester. As he was trying to escape Peace once more took out a revolver and shot poor PC Nicholas Cock, who unfortunately died the day after of his injuries. Once more Peace was able to escape; and two brothers who lived near to the scene were later arrested and charged with the killing. One of them was acquitted for lack of evidence but the other was initially sentenced to death; but this was later commuted to penal servitude for the rest of his life.

During his time in Darnall Peace had developed an obsessive interest in a Mrs Dyson, but she spurned his attentions. As a result of this, and knowing that he was a violent man, the Dyson family moved to another part of Sheffield called Banner Cross but it wasn't long before Peace found out where they lived and started once more to harass them. After an argument between Peace and Mrs Dyson, Mr Dyson, who had heard the commotion, started to chase Peace away from the scene. At the same time Peace once more drew a revolver and turned and killed Mr Dyson with a shot through the head. Peace had been seen in the suburb of Banner Cross by several people but he somehow managed to escape to Hull where he had family.

Seemingly at some time or other he left Hull and ended up in London where once more he became a prolific and successful burglar in the affluent suburb of Blackheath.

The termination of this profitable crime spree ended on the 10th October 1878 when he was caught breaking into a house in St John's Park. Once more as he was trying to make his escape, he drew his revolver and fired four shots at the policemen who were trying to apprehend him. One of the police officers, a contable Robinson, was hit by a bullet which passed completely through his arm but nevertheless he was able to detain Peace. He was remanded in custody for a week and refused to give his identity; and it was only when he wrote a letter to an old colleague who then alerted the police as to who he was that he admitted the offence. For this crime Peace was sentenced to servitude for life for the attempted murder of the brave PC Robinson.

At the time of arrest the police had taken possession of the revolver which Peace had used in trying to evade apprehension. Examination of the revolver and the rifling on the bullet fired at PC Robinson also linked Peace to both the murder of Mr Dyson in Sheffield and PC Cock in Manchester. Because of this Peace was taken back to Sheffield and committed to stand trial at Leeds Assizes where he received the death penalty. At that point, having nothing to lose, he readily admitted the murder of PC Cock in Manchester and the two brothers who had unfortunately been arrested for Cock's death were exonerated. Peace's execution – death by hanging – was carried out in Armley Gaol, Leeds on 25th February 1879.

Peace had gained so much notoriety throughout the country that a depiction of him and the executioner, William Marwood, became a waxwork in the Chamber of Horrors in Madam Tussaud's, London – what a nasty piece of work he was, no wonder people used to threaten their kids with him; he was still infamous eighty years later.

The other thing that I used to hear when I first arrived as a 'rookie' pc, were comments from both the public and some of the old bobbies about the famous Sheffield Gang Wars, some of the descendants of which lived in the Attercliffe area where I worked. Since being a kid I've always had a big interest in local history and so once more I started to delve in order to find out what the Sheffield Gang Wars was all about.

In the 1920s, after the First World War, the country was at peace once more. For Sheffield this resulted in a large drop in the output of steel which had been required for the war effort, and now there were a huge amount of people unemployed, including ex-soldiers returning from the war and who now needed to make a living. There being no work available, a lot of people turned to both petty and serious crime to support themselves; and this included some ex-soldiers. Having committed a crime it was easy to disappear into the labyrinth of the rat-infested slum streets of Sheffield as they were then. Having gained a few quid from crimes such as theft, house breaking, pick-pocketing or extortion, the criminals needed an outlet for the money that they had stolen.

Enter George Mooney, gangster.

George Mooney ran the pitch and toss betting ring on Sky Edge, near to City Road above Sheffield; and huge amounts of money would change hands.* One of the big players was a publican from Barnsley called Jack White who would gamble £50 just on the throw of a coin – a massive amount of money in those days. Hundreds of people would gather both to take part and to watch this highly lucrative but illegal undertaking; and every time the game was played George Mooney would take a kick back of 20 per cent. This money was to pay for the 'tollers' (the people who collected in the money) and 'pickers and crows' (people who were at a vantage point looking out for the police arrival). If the police did arrive, which they often did, the gamblers and their cronies would flee the scene, taking with them any evidence to do with the tossing ring. After the war came the depression and because of this the fall in Mooney's earnings dropped like a stone. This caused him to dispose of some of his workers, including minders and enforcers; and so they themselves decided to set up a rival gang called the Park Brigade.

Enter Sam Garvin, the head of the Park Brigade.

Sam Garvin was a career criminal having been in prison many times for assault, illegal gaming, theft and con tricks. He also

---

* Pitch and toss was played by someone placing three pennies on the tips of their three upward-pointing fingers. These coins were then tossed into the air and people gambled on the number of heads or tails that were facing up when landing back on the ground.

ran illegal pub yard bare knuckle boxing matches – not just in Sheffield but all over the country; and was a well-known figure to the criminal communities throughout the land.

Garvin was so well-known in Sheffield – or more than likely feared – that when the first few council houses became available he was able to obtain one of them. At that time the slums were being knocked down and he ought to have been the last man to have been given one rather than the first. Can you imagine a council house being given to a man who drove a green 3-litre Bentley saloon car around the streets of Sheffield? What was the council thinking about?, wink wink!

At that point in time you had two gangs vying to run the city's criminal activities: 1 – George Mooney and 2 – Sam Garvin. Violence and confrontation was inevitable. Both men wanted all of the action and not just a part of it. The Sheffield Gang Wars were about to take place resulting in Sheffield being called 'Little Chicago' by the press.

The first gang attack was organized by Mooney's mob when they invaded the home of William Furniss, a member of the Park Brigade. Furniss was in bed when he was attacked and was severely injured by a host of blows from hammers. Despite this he did not report the matter to the police. Furniss wasn't interested in justice – only revenge. As a reprisal for the Furniss beating one of Mooney's minders, Frank Kidnew, was slashed with a cut-throat razor more than a hundred times, near Sky Edge. He was taken to the hospital but he would not make a complaint to the police; and it is said that he was more worried about his ruined suit being slashed and covered in blood than about himself. He defiantly told the police, 'I reckon it's spoiled my suit.'

A while later the Park Brigade retaliated by attacking their main adversary George Mooney himself, at his home. One of the attackers was shot in the shoulder and when the police arrived they found a double-barrelled shot gun, a rifle, revolver and ammunition. For being in possession of firearms he was fined the paltry sum of £10.

After that Mooney's home was attacked on various occasions when several people, including policemen, needed medical attention.

One Christmas Eve the Park Brigade, including Sam Garvin the leader, again smashed into Mooney's home where they terrorized his wife and six children. It had been their intention to slash Mooney up with cut-throat razors but he had managed to escape by hiding in a cupboard. Not surprisingly Mooney then abandoned Sheffield, leaving his gang to fend for themselves.

Garvin had won but instead of enjoying his new found reputation and illegal business interests he got involved with a pointless killing in Princess Street, Attercliffe.

William Plommer was a 34-year-old Scottish ex-soldier and a labourer in the steel works; and had no connection with either Garvin, Mooney or crime whatsoever. The exact reason why he was attacked is not known but over the last sixty odd years since then there have been several theories that have been put forward as to why; but I'm sure that the truth will never be known. What is certain is that Garvin himself, the two Fowler brothers, along with eight or ten others, tracked Plommer through the streets of Sheffield. When they found him they were joined by as many as twenty-five other people who all made the assault on Plommer. Although Plommer was unarmed, he stood his ground like a man and the soldier that he had once been, but for all his bravery he was beaten unmercifully to the floor with coshes, pokers and fists, along with chair legs which had been hollowed out and filled with lead. His injuries were both shocking and appalling and as he was crawling through the streets on his hands and knees trying to get back to his home the heavy beatings continued unabated – he didn't stand a chance.

Eventually some people came to his aid and it was found that Plommer had not only got severe head injuries but also two huge wounds, apparently caused by having a bayonet thrust through his stomach and side. He was taken to the Royal Infirmary a short distance away but died only minutes later.

When the ambulance left with Plommer some of the gang members, including the two Fowler brothers, sat around on the steps of a shop near to where they had beaten Plommer to death; and on arrival of the police Laurence Fowler readily admitted to hitting Plommer on the head. Both were taken to the police station and when told that Plommer's injuries were serious Laurence denied striking him on the head. Sam Garvin, who thought he was smarter than the rest, immediately after the beating had jumped on a tram and travelled some distance to the city before jumping off it and assaulting the first man that he saw, thinking that this would give him an alibi. He wasn't as smart as he thought and he and nine others including the Fowler brothers were taken to the police station.

This senseless murder caused a huge hue and cry nationally and John Hall-Dalwood, who was the Chief Constable at that time, received orders from the Home Office to crack down on gang violence by forming the Special Duty Squad, or Flying Squad, of four police officers with instructions to smash the gang's activities. The first Squad was set up and contained four of the biggest and toughest men in the police force, their leader being an ex-Cold Stream Guard, Sergeant Robinson. Another was a 6' 2" and 20 stone ex-Royal Artillery man called Walter Loxley. A third was PC Herbert Lunn who had been awarded bravery medals for saving his comrades whilst under heavy fire in the war; and the last was Jack Farrily who, prior to joining the police, had made a decent living as a street fighter.

For political reasons, John Hall-Dalwood was later told to resign and his job was taken over by Percy Sillitoe, whose first recruit for his newly formed squad was PC Pat Geraghty, a giant of a man standing 6' 5" tall. The European Ju-Jitsu champion Harry Hunter then spent several weeks training these men in self-defence to help them deal with any form of attack. It is said that this squad would throw criminals through doors and windows without opening them first; and they would often beat up criminals in public view in order to teach others a lesson.

Pub landlords were instructed by this Flying Squad not to serve any gang members whatsoever or they would lose their licence.

Prior to leaving the force the previous Chief Constable, Hall-Dalwood, had publically said that the problems of gang warfare were as a result of both a lack of police presence on the streets and a lack of prosecution in the judicial system. The punishments weren't a deterrent to the crimes, which meant that it paid to be a criminal; and that Sheffield, because of this, was producing criminals as good as the steel that the city was famous for; he also said that the prosecutors were under pressure from the gangs; and that some of the police were corrupt. Is it any wonder that Sheffield had gained the dubious nickname of 'Little Chicago'?

Altogether, ten men went to trial accused of causing or aiding in Plommer's murder and these included the Fowler brothers and the leader Sam Garvin. The murder weapon, the bayonet, was never found but several witnesses said that it had been wielded by Wilfred Fowler and his brother Laurence, who was said to have used a truncheon. At the end of the trial three men: George Wills, Stanley Harker and Amos Stewart, were each sentenced to twenty-seven years for manslaughter; and the leader, Sam Garvin, received twenty months for the assault he had committed to give himself an alibi. The judge sentenced the two Fowler brothers to death for murder and on Friday 4th September 1925 Wilfred was hanged in Armley Prison, Leeds. Due to new evidence, his brother Laurence appealed but the Home Secretary rejected his appeal and he was also hanged. About 10,000 people attended Plommer's funeral – the whole nation was in shock. The law later also caught up with the old gang leader George Mooney when he was sent to gaol for biting off a man's ear on the way back from a racecourse.

From Sheffield, Sillitoe was sent up to Glasgow to deal with the 'razor gangs' and he then went on to become head of MI5 during which time he dealt with the threat of Communist spying; and also exposed the Cambridge Spy Ring consisting of Philby and Burgess. From there he went on to become the Head of the International Diamond Security Organisation where he managed to stop diamond smuggling from Sierra Leone. He died in the south of England, aged 73.

Tough men in tough situations need to be very flexible, a word that I found to be quite apt when as a young police constable, I looked around the police black museum where I saw what at first I thought to be a black walking stick. It was amongst other mementoes of the gang wars including pistols, cut throat razors, various knuckle dusters, coshes, socks with lumps of lead in them, a club with nails in the end and a chair leg full of lead. All these weapons were used during the Gang Wars; and so I asked an old sergeant Rip Rollins, what the walking stick was for. I was amazed at his reply.

'That's a bull's penis or "pizzle",' he said. 'The gang busters would go to the abattoir and obtain one. It would then be hung in a cellar with a strong wire threaded through the tube inside it. It would be hung with weights hanging from it in order to make it straight and at the same time it would be covered with saltpetre and dried to make it hard as well as flexible. It had then been used by the gang busters as a weapon against the gangs.

Eventually, the gangs were dispersed and the outbreak of the Second World War brought a further boost to Sheffield's steel industry; and so once again there was very little unemployment which brought both wealth and peace back to the city once more.

CHAPTER 11

A Sprat to Catch a Mackerel

Human nature is a funny thing and luckily for us we are all very different from each other. As policemen we encountered people from all walks of life and backgrounds; and the areas in which I worked contained working-class houses and working-class people, just the way I liked it – nothing fancy.

People used to say that if you were a policeman you would never have any friends; what a load of rubbish; if you were right with them then they would be right with you. We cared about people and their safety and especially those who were being bullied and couldn't defend themselves.

Over the last couple of months both Rick, John and myself had been getting feedback from our favourite watering hole that Marlene, the prostitute, was getting beaten on a regular basis by Mr Nasty Pimp, the sadistic pillock who ran her and three other girls. More often than not the people who get involved in prostitution do so by choice and for their own reasons. Marlene's case, however, was very different – she'd been forced into it and was now being used as a commodity by the bully boy.

He was obviously a nasty piece of work who, as far as we were aware, had never legally worked; and to make matters more annoying still, when I discreetly checked with the dole office on West Street, I discovered that he was also on the dole. So not content with making a good living off the earnings of four prostitutes who he beat up on a regular basis, he also had the nerve to claim benefits as well. Apart from living off immoral earnings and claiming the dole none of us could abide or respect violent thugs who beat up women. Time for some action.

The offence of living off immoral earnings was a difficult one to prove, mainly because the four girls were already in fear of violence and would not make a complaint. Mr Nasty Pimp's method of operation was to wait outside the block of flats where the girls used to take their clients in order to give them a good time. When the client left – skint but happy, and hoping that he hadn't caught a dose of something – Mr Nasty Pimp would nip upstairs and grab all the money off whichever girl had done the business. She would then be made to go back on the streets and would be required to attract another client as quickly as possible. This would go on all day or night until she had met her imposed target; and if she didn't achieve that target then she would get beaten up in such a way so as not to be marked. If she was marked on her face then her customers would be put off and go elsewhere. This was the regime that he imposed on all 'his' girls.

This was the added danger to any prostitute if she got herself into the clutches of a pimp. The pimp would constantly keep them short of money so that they relied on his hand outs and by doing this he kept them as virtual prisoners; and they couldn't find a way to escape from it.

As we all know there are more ways to skin a cat than one, and the odd thing is that the more you get to know people, including the prostitutes, you also became, somehow, more protective towards them; and at least try to keep them out of harm's way. Being unable to prove anything officially without getting the girls' consent or getting them into further trouble was very frustrating. At one stage Rick and I decided to take the law into our own hands and lay in wait for Mr Nasty Pimp at the bottom of the stairs in the dark lobby in the block of flats that they used and then to have a gentle man-to-man chat with him. This was obviously not a good idea as we, ourselves, would have more than likely ended up in bother, so what were we to do?

Without mentioning a word to Marlene, just in case she let something slip and gave the game away, Rick and I went to our favourite watering hole, the one that we'd nicknamed 'Mucky Mary's'. We had a discreet chat with one or two of the girls who were prostitutes, but who worked alone. The girls were aware of Marlene's plight and were all very willing to help in doing something about it. They knew Mr Nasty Pimp and the way he treated 'his girls'. He even made them work when they were 'unwell'. He was a disgusting pig of a bloke.

The snare was set but would the bait be taken? Only time would tell.

The following week Rick, John and I were on the afternoon shift, 3pm to 11pm and sometime in the early evening having dealt with some other enquiries, we nipped into Mucky Mary's for a glass of beer. As was usual by now, the first half was bought by one of the lads in the snug, who upon our arrival into the pub all shouted, 'One, two, three CID,' and all blew us a kiss. It always caused a laugh and we joined in, what a crowd, they were brilliant.

About fifteen minutes later you could hear the phone ringing in the outside telephone kiosk and I thought to myself that that must be business for one of the girls. Alan, the barman, went out to answer it. In less than a minute Alan poked his head round the door, and said: 'Janice on the phone for you Rick.' And with that Rick went outside and came back a minute later.

'Interesting, what's he up to?' I thought, knowing that Janice was one of the prostitutes.

When he came back into the pub he grabbed and polished off his glass of beer and I did the same, knowing that we were probably on the trail of Mr Nasty Pimp and with that we were in the car and off to one of the lower-class pubs in the city where Janice had told Rick that she had seen Mr Nasty Pimp going into. Sure enough, there he was propping up the bar and talking to what was thought to be a small-time drug dealer.

The pub was fairly busy with 'likely lads' and one or two villains who all knew who we were and I had to smile as one or two of them scuttled out of the back door.

'Two halves, landlord please', I asked loudly, 'and a pint for my pal over there leaning on the bar (the pimp).' As the landlord passed him his pint you could see him ask where it had come from; and as the landlord pointed to Rick and I, in full view of the rest of the pub, our man, with a puzzled look on his face, muttered 'Thanks, cheers lads.'

With that we quickly supped our beer and as we were leaving Rick lifted his thumb up in the air, looked across at Mr Nasty Pimp and shouted, 'Cheers for last night, pal, you were spot on!' The look of astonishment on his face was amazing.

A couple of nights later John and Rick were in Mucky Mary's when 'the phone call' came again and so they were able to repeat the scenario in a different lower-class pub, frequented by different villains. The scenario was very similar and the conversation the same, apart from that it was John who did the thumbs up and the thanks. The look on Mr Nasty Pimp's face had been similar to that of a few nights before. He couldn't reckon up what was happening, but more importantly for us, the other people that he was with couldn't understand what was happening either.

In the first week we managed to carry out the same scenario three times in different pubs and in front of different villains including some of the medium players in the scrap business. He must have wondered what the hell we were up to and it made us chuckle thinking about what was going through his mind.

Three weeks later when we were on afters again and because he was a creature of habit we found him in the same pubs; and we did exactly the same as we had done before. Buying him a pint, shouting across to thank him and then leaving him. By this stage he looked really rattled and also angry.

After the second week we discreetly asked one of the girls, Janice, whether Marlene was okay and was the same thing happening? She told us that Marlene had been slapped around a bit but thankfully nothing serious.

It was to be another three weeks before we were on afters again and during that week we visited the same three pubs that he used; but we purposely visited them when we knew, from the girls, that he WOULDN'T be in. In each pub we would stand at the bar quietly and slowly, instead of swiftly, drink our half of beer rather than rushing it as we had done before. All eyes were on us and you could see that the likely lads and villains were wondering why we were there. None of the three pubs were where we would usually go for a pint, so what was going off?

Was our plan working? Let's see.

All three pubs contained hard men who didn't mess about and seeing that some of them were in I nipped to the toilet to see what would happen. Sure enough I was followed in by a bloke who had been in bother for handling stolen metal and was also one of the men that had been standing next to Mr Nasty Pimp on one of our visits.

'All right Mr Johnson?' he asked, 'you're getting a bit regular in here aren't you?'

'Aye, I was hoping to have a chat with a pal of mine, I owe him a pint or two, but I can see that he's not in.' I answered. 'I'll catch him next time.' With that I walked out and we left the pub – perfect.

Rick and John did the same in the other pubs, the cogs in the underworld would be working overtime – we hoped. We had to wait another three weeks before we were on afters again in order to find out whether our plan had worked.

We were very busy for the first three days of our afternoon shift and it was Thursday before we had the chance to call in at Mary's, where as usual, we were greeted with, 'One, two, three CID,' from the lads in the tap room and oddly enough two of the girls in the other room did the same. At the same time Cecil said, 'I'll get those two halves.' But before he had chance to do so Janice rushed to the bar and said, 'No you won't, I'll get them tonight.'

'That's very kind of you Janice and most unusual,' laughed Rick, 'what's that for?'

'What's that for, what's that for?' Janice said, 'I'll tell you what it's for. He's f-----g gone, gentlemen. That's what it's for.'

She was obviously excited and Rick and I had obviously worked out what she was talking about but we decided to play along.

'Who's gone Janice, what are you talking about?' Rick said.

'That bastard who's been hitting Marlene, that's who's gone and Marlene's safe at last and working with us lot, she'll be okay. I don't know how you did it but well done.'

At that point, Stella, the other girl who was fairly new and a beauty, walked up to me and Rick, put her arms round our necks and said, as she flashed loads of flesh, 'The treat's on me tonight lads, if you want to come back to the flat.' And we all laughed together.

Two minutes later in walked Jennie, one of the older girls along with Marlene who looked a totally different person. She had spruced herself up and was far more relaxed and self-assured than when we'd last seen her. On seeing Rick and me she looked at us both and slowly started to cry, her tears were spoiling her mascara and it was running down her cheeks. Through the sobs she said, 'I don't know how you've done it but he's gone and at last I feel safe.' As Jennie was comforting her we asked what had happened.

'He's been acting very odd this last week or two and he became very shifty; and he was looking round him all the time as if someone was after him. When I asked him what was the matter he wouldn't tell me but just grabbed the money I'd made and fled – two days ago he stumbled into the flat with his left arm in a sling and he was limping badly. His face was covered in bruises and a couple of his teeth were missing and he was mumbling that some men had told him that he was a police informant and then gave him a bit of a beating, at the same time telling him to leave Town or he'd get some more. He grabbed some clothes and he was off and I've not seen him since – and I don't want to either. I thought he would end up killing me.'

It was pretty obvious to us that one of the girls must have told Marlene that we'd been asking after Mr Nasty Pimp's whereabouts but we didn't elaborate or make her any the wiser.

About six weeks later the new girl, Stella, whispered to me that she thought she'd seen 'our man' in Town, so the following day I, once more, contacted the dole office only to be told that he was now collecting his dole money at the Ipswich office which proved that he was at last out of our hair. I phoned the CID office in Ipswich and outlined the situation; and told them of his background; and to keep an eye out for him as he was violent towards women.

Right from me being a nipper I've always sided with the underdog. I'd cheer on the Indians instead of the cowboys and loved it when Popeye ate his spinach and got his own back against the bully boy. I've never been impressed by people who try to impress me but I've always been impressed by people who, although sometimes unfortunate themselves, give of their time and their efforts to help other people without making a fuss about it and have nothing to gain themselves for doing so. I guess it was the way I was brought up.

Prostitutes, male or female, have often been brought up in poor surroundings and poor conditions and do what they do to try and earn an honest crust. It is said that prostitution is the oldest profession in the world and many people have tried to stamp it out because it is an offence to human nature. It is also a 'profession' that, in my opinion and that of many other policemen, will never cease to exist and it would be far better if, like in some other countries, it was legalized. At that point they can have health checks and there would be no Mr Nasty Pimps about.

Historically and currently you only have to read the newspapers or watch the media to discover how many politicians, bankers or business people have been brought to heel having been caught using the services of prostitutes, to know that it is common throughout the world.

If people (men or women) have got the brass to pay a good looking and willing girl or man for sex, then that is what they'll do and no questions asked. All these people as well as being able to afford to pay, must have got, in their minds, a genuine need for doing so in the first place. It may be as a result of a partner dying, lack of confidence or just purely and simply for sexual gratification, but whatever the reason and no matter how many times you try to sweep it under the carpet, it will never go away.

Legalized brothels, run by the government would ensure health checks for whoever, safety for the clients and safety for the prostitutes involved. You only have to look back over the last few years at the Yorkshire Ripper and the murderer of several prostitutes in Ipswich to make sense of what I have just said. For a little while I even wondered whether the perpetrator of the Ipswich murders could have been connected with Mr Nasty Pimp, until I realized that he would probably be too old.

A few years after I'd left the police force, Jennie, one of the older girls, unfortunately passed away (the one who had given me a pre-natal midwifery lesson [see *What's Tha Up To This Time?*]) and through Attercliffe Police Station the other girls sought Rick and me out to tell us of her passing. Rick and I were honoured at their request for us to attend Jennie's funeral. By this time Mucky Mary's had been knocked down; but it was lovely to once more meet up with the old crowd that we had known so well and had laughed and had such good times with. Unbelievably, when we arrived outside the church you could hear quiet whispers from different people: 'One, two, three CID'.

After the funeral we all got together and talked about the good times that we had spent in Mucky Mary's.

I have no idea just how good she was at her profession but what I can tell you is that Jennie was a wonderful, happy, caring person and worthy of our respect.

Anyway enough of being serious, let's have a bit of fun.

CHAPTER 12

'Taka Me Down to De Ceee I Deee'

On the job that we were on you never knew from one minute to the next what you were going to deal with – it could be absolutely anything. Neither did you know what sort of people you were going to meet. In Attercliffe we were never invited to grand parties or fancy houses, that was left to the bobbies at the opposite side of the city where the posher people lived.

I often asked myself how I ended up working in Attercliffe, the rougher end of the city, even though after a while I got used to it and loved the characters that lived there.

When I left school at the age of fifteen I'd anticipated working down the pit, the same as almost everyone else did in the Barnsley area, including my own dad, granddad and great granddad had done before me. When I told this to my dad he went absolutely crackers, saying 'No son of mine is going darn't pit, it's too dangerous.'

I knew what he meant because he'd twice before been buried alive by a roof fall deep down in the mine. On one of those occasions the local policeman had woken us in the middle of the night. Mum was crying as she dragged my little sister, Bronnie, and myself, aged about five, through the darkness of the two-mile walk to Houghton Main Colliery where dad was working the night shift. We waited at the pit top along with other mums and children, all of whom were crying wondering if they would see their husbands or dads again. After what seemed like hours the pit rescue teams travelled up from the bowels of the earth in the 'cage'. We'd all been lucky that night as dad and several other men were rescued and then rushed to the hospital, they were all alive but injured.

After a couple of weeks in hospital and a week or two in the Miners' Convalescent Home near Scarborough, dad was able to go back to work again, but the experience had really shaken him up big style.

I ended up working as a blacksmith's and sheet metalworker's apprentice near to where I lived; and at the age of nineteen the local vicar, a lovely man called Reverend Howard, got me to sign some papers applying to become a policeman in Sheffield.

Like me there were young lads of about nineteen and also ex-soldiers applying for the job. Unlike most of the other lads there I had no academic qualifications whatsoever, but nevertheless, and somehow, we all managed to pass the exam (which I think must have been a foregone conclusion in those days).

After three months training at Pannal Ash Police Training School in Harrogate the officer in charge had to decide which division within the Sheffield boundary that we would be sent to work in.

Looking me up and down he asked me one question: 'Can you fight lad?'

'Yes, sir,' I said, not daring to say any other, even though I could fight (you have to when you come from Barnsley). At that point the senior officer looked at everyone else in the room, sniggered and said, 'It looks, then, that we've got someone for Attercliffe.' At that point the rest of the lads, who obviously knew the city better than me, burst out laughing

I wondered why the lads had laughed but I soon found out when I got to Attercliffe, it was a totally, totally different world to the one I was used to.

After a while I got used to the volume of people who lived and worked there along with the amount of vehicles, something I wasn't used to seeing where I lived in Darfield. It was trial by fire and at first I wondered what had hit me. But the place was full of wonderful people and characters. So that's how I ended up working down the 'Cliffe and after working down there for many years I wouldn't have wanted to work anywhere else in the city; I'd got used to it.

Some eight years later there I was with Rick who was driving the CID car down Pitsmoor Rd, near to the old Tollgate Cottage. As we joined Barnsley Road and passed the famous Mojo club we could see a commotion taking place near the Sportsman pub. A few people were gathered around two middle-aged black men who were pushing each other about. One of them was known to us as being a petty thief; and just as we pulled up in the car we saw him pull out a knife from somewhere or other and wave it about in a threatening manner towards the other bloke's face.

As Rick and I jumped out of the car Rick shouted, 'Police – put that knife down on the floor!' which made the man hesitate. He knew who we were and there was a resigned look on his face as we got near to him, but right at the last second he turned towards the other bloke; and more in an act of petulance rather than anger, he caught the back of the man's hand with the point of the knife. At the same time I leapt on his back and put him in a strangle hold; and the knife fell to the floor from where Rick picked it up.

The man didn't struggle at all and simply said, 'Okay, Mr Hardwick, okay. That man made me cross,' and he pointed to the other bloke.

The other man, who was a friend of the assailant, had only suffered a superficial cut to his hand so we took his details and arrested Mr Blade and put him in the back of the CID car where I sat with him for safety reasons. We then set off to Attercliffe police station with him.

After a couple of minutes into our journey Mr Blade, unbelievably, started to sing in something similar to a Calypso voice. *What the bloody hell is he singing about*, I thought – *he's under arrest*.

I could see Rick's face in the interior mirror and he had a puzzled expression on it the same as mine. The next few minutes were one of the oddest and funniest situations I have ever been in as I listened to the man start singing again in his Calypso-style way.

This is what he sang:

'*Mr Hardwick* (and he paused for 10 seconds)
he taka meee (another 10-second pause).
He taka meee down to de Ceee I Deeee, (pause)
and there he'll interview meee, (10-second pause)
and then he basha mee you see.'

And then in a gleeful sing song voice he finished up chuckling and then sang '*And then he'll give me a cuppa teeee*'.

Through the interior mirror Rick and I looked at each other in absolute amazement and then we set off laughing big style. It was one of the funniest things I had ever heard; and the words and the way he sung them have never left me after over forty odd years. We were still laughing as we led him upstairs to the CID office where we sat him down and I mashed all three of us a pot of tea with tears of laughter running down my cheeks.

'What were you and your mate arguing about anyway?' asked Rick.

'He say that my wife was a big fat cow,' and he paused and then said, 'I know she's a cow but she's not as fat as he said, and it *mada* me cross.'

At that point Rick and I collapsed with laughter, we couldn't do a thing. Mr Blade was also laughing. He was so relaxed and laid back, you couldn't help but like him. His laughter was so infectious and Rick and I were just beside ourselves. It was one of the funniest interviews we'd ever had. He had no previous convictions for violence and so we decided to take him back with us to have a word with his mate.

We spoke to his mate who wouldn't make a complaint against him and he said that they were good friends really. His injury didn't warrant hospital treatment and was only a scratch. As it was a minor offence we decided to report him on summons instead of locking him up. He only lived a few streets away and so we decided to drop him off at his home and low and behold he started to slowly sing once more:

'*Mr Johnson* (pause) *he maka me* (pause)
a lovely cuppa teeee (pause).
And now he taka me home you seeee (long pause).
I been a naughty boy today (pause) *And de magistrate will maka me payyy*'

As we were dropping the man off outside his house his wife came out through the front door to meet him, with a face like thunder. I turned and looked at Rick and he looked at me. We couldn't get away fast enough and as we turned for our last look at Mr Blade he put his arms out with his palms upwards, looked up at the sky with a resigned look on his face as if to say, 'Help me'. His wife must have been eighteen or nineteen stone in weight and she was seething mad. Once again Rick and I cracked up laughing and we did so for weeks afterwards. Now you know why I say that anything can happen on our job. One minute we're dealing with an angry man wielding a knife and in the next few minutes we're laughing our heads off with him – it was amazing.

As we once more drove past the Mojo club I started to chuckle and shake my head at the same time as I remembered it for two reasons. In 1963 Peter Stringfellow, the same man that now owns Stringfellows Night Club in London, owned the Mojo and the Azena Night Club. Peter, being a good Sheffield lad and very astute, had booked a group to perform at the Azena. At that time no one really knew the group who hailed from Liverpool and called themselves the Beatles. They turned out to be a sensation and I am sure that they are now known to every single person in the world.

A couple of months after the Beatles' visit I was invited by the local youth club leader at Handsworth Church to a dance at the church hall. He wanted to introduce the local bobby to the youngsters at the club, in order for us to get to know each other better. Good for him what a good idea, I thought.

It was a lot busier than I imagined it would be, and as far as I can remember it was an annual event in celebration of something or other. I envied the young chap who was playing the rubbing board in the skiffle band, which is what I used to play in our little band back home. The youngsters were all bopping and jiving away to music by Bill Haley, Little Richard and the Everly Brothers. I'd have loved to join in but having been invited to attend in an official capacity meant that I wouldn't have stood a chance trying to bop in a pair of heavy police boots. I chatted with loads of the lads who were wearing their drainpipe trousers and beetle-crusher shoes. 'Ducks arse' haircuts were all the rage then and even I had one, accompanied by a Brylcreamed quiff at the front.

The girls, just like the lads, were dolled up to the nines.

There were loads of raffle prizes to be won and these had been donated by various people and local businesses. During one of the intervals the youth leader asked if I would go on stage to draw out the winning tickets, which had been folded up and put into a bank money bag, made out of cloth. To save any argy-bargy and time wasting the youth leader had earlier numbered the prizes from 1 to 27, so the first number out of the bag had prize number one and so on. He then announced that the star prize (number 1) was a signed LP record by Roy Orbison. I then drew out the winning ticket and everyone clapped the young girl who had won the prize. Prize number 2 was tickets to a Sheffield Wednesday match but it was for the Directors Box which caused excitement amongst some of the lads but boos from the Sheffield United fans. Luckily the winner was a Sheffield Wednesday supporter anyway. The youth club leader then held up the third prize, a signed album, photograph and a poster from the recent Beatles gig in Sheffield and all signed by the lads with the funny haircuts. As the girls started to scream you could see the looks of amazement on the youth leader's face. He'd obviously never heard of the Beatles and it was only because I'd read about them in the *Sheffield Star* newspaper that the name meant anything to me. At that time they weren't as famous as they are now or it would have obviously been the first and star prize.

There was a hush in the room as the youth leader held the large cloth bag whilst I rummaged round inside it for a ticket. I'll never forget the number, it was 196, the collar number of my mate down the 'Cliffe, Walter Damms. As I announced the number and held it up in the air everyone checked their tickets – no response. I shouted, '196,' again but no response so I suggested to the youth leader that maybe we should have another draw.

'Didn't I see you buy some tickets when you came in tonight?' he asked me.

'Blimey, you're right. Four strips of them,' I replied.

Opening the breast pocket of my uniform I took out my pocket book into which I'd put my tickets earlier and then I passed them over for him to check. I felt a right twerp when he held up the ticket 196 and announced that PC Johnson was the winner! I even offered to return the prize but he wouldn't hear anything of it. Most people clapped but I had to chuckle as I received a few jeers from the girls and 'fixed!' from the boys. I felt terrible and embarrassed that I'd won the prize.

The raffle of about thirty prizes had made quite a lot of money for the Youth Club and I was pleased that I'd been asked to be involved. As I left the stage with my prize a small crowd of young girls rushed up to me, eager to see what I had won. They were all excited and some even offered to buy the items off me, the highest offer being £2 which would have been a fair amount of money then, but I told them that they weren't for sale and off they went back to the dance floor. One of the young girls had caught my attention. She was quieter than the other girls had been and for some reason she also looked very sad and withdrawn. Half an hour later I had the opportunity to speak with her because I couldn't stop thinking about why she looked so sad.

'Have you enjoyed the dance tonight? I asked her.

'Yes it's been very good,' she replied and looked down at the floor.

'You don't look very happy, are you all right?' I gently asked, trying to make conversation. There was obviously something wrong and I thought it might help if she talked about it. She obviously didn't want to so I left her on her own. I made it in my way to ask one of the other girls what her problem was and they told me that she had wanted to go to the Beatles concert with them at the Azena but that there had been an accident at one of the steel works and her dad had been seriously injured and had died the day before the concert. Her dad had bought her and her sister tickets for the concert but they just couldn't face going in the circumstances. How sad for her to have to go through something so terrible as losing her dad at such a young age, and I remembered how we felt when my dad was buried alive down the pit.

I didn't want to embarrass the girl further so, before I went back to my lodgings, I asked the youth leader if he would pass on the Beatles prize to the young girl in the hope that it made her feel a bit better. I often wish that I'd kept them, they would now be worth a fortune, but the sad look on that young girl's face that night made it all worthwhile. I hope she's still got them but if you happen to read this and you've sold them, don't forget you owe me a pint.

A good few years after the Beatles' visit to Sheffield I was on foot patrol duty near Pitsmoor and I had been asked to rendezvous with the Warrants Officer, a lovely bloke called Jack Silkstone. Jack travelled all over the city serving warrants or summonses on people who had failed to turn up at court. From what Jack told me when we met up, the Mojo club had closed down but he'd received information that a young chap was living in the building and that he was wanted for something or other. Jack had been a couple of times on previous occasions and tried to serve the summons but had been unsuccessful. On both occasions there had been lights on in the top of the building and whoever the young chap was, he had not answered the door and Jack suspected that he had exited through the back of the house.

Jack's request to me was quite simple. Could I stand at the back of the premises while he knocked on the front door? Sure enough on our arrival we could see lights on in the top of the building and so I tiptoed round to the back door. As it was winter time and in the evening it was very dark so I was able to hide in the shadows. After a few minutes I could hear what sounded like a transom window being opened above me and realized that Jack must have knocked on the door alerting the man inside. I must have been right because a few seconds later a young chap came sliding down a drainpipe at which point I grabbed his collar and told him that he was under arrest.

I didn't know the lad from Adam but I did know that he wasn't one of the Stringfellow brothers because I'd been fortunate to meet them once before. I never did get to know what he was wanted for but Jack arrested him and took him away.

Footnote: We all like a success story and it's great to know that Peter Stringfellow, a local man, has done so well for himself. About three or four years ago I read in *The Times* that Peter had insisted on giving back to the government his winter fuel allowance because he didn't need it. Well done Peter – you're a proper Sheffield 'Mester'.

CHAPTER 13

What a Night

The day had started off okay and as I slowly crawled out from under the covers I could see that daylight was shining in through the bedroom curtains. With only one eye open I looked at the bedside clock – 8.30am – I jumped out of bed in a panic, I should be at work for nine. At the same time as I was running to the bathroom I shouted downstairs to Christine: 'Christine, get my snap ready, love quick, I'm late for work.'

'You're on nights you dozy thing, it's your first shift starting tonight,' Christine shouted; and I could hear her laughing downstairs.

Panic over, so I jumped back into bed and snuggled in, it was a freezing cold day. No peace for the wicked I discovered as Christine plonked our one-year-old son Richard on the bed with me. After a fantastic half an hour of fun with my lad we got up and had a late breakfast before party time.

It would be a first for us – not many people reached their 100th birthday in those days, but today was one of them. At 1pm we attended our friend Alma Oscroft's mum's centenary birthday, which had been arranged by Alma and her daughter Jean and son-in-law Roy at Wath-upon-Dearne. Mrs Wood was a lovely lady who went on to be 105 years of age. At 4pm we then attended my one-year-old niece Lucy's birthday party in Barnsley. It was an odd experience celebrating two birthdays in one afternoon and with 99 years between their ages.

When I went to work that evening at 10.30pm I decided to leave my best suit on instead of faffing about getting changed. Sundays on night shift were usually fairly quiet, so I was hoping to catch up with the dreaded part of the job – the ball-aching paperwork. Armed with a pint pot of tea and an ash tray I set about my tedious task. All was going well until the duty sergeant in the downstairs office telephoned me. 'A woman's just come into the station with her son who she says has been shop lifting,' he said.

'Shop lifting – its half past midnight, the shops have been closed for hours,' I replied in amazement. 'Okay, I'll come down to see them.'

When I got downstairs and into the main office I could see a youngish woman of about forty who looked both upset and angry. Standing beside her was a lad of about sixteen to seventeen years of age who looked scared to death when he saw me and realized who I was. I took them both upstairs to the CID office, sat them down and asked the lady to tell me what the problem was. She wasn't happy at all.

'Late yesterday evening I went up to my sons bedroom to make his bed and when I opened a cupboard in order to get a clean pillow case, I found four packets of ten Park Drive cigarettes and six bars of chocolate,' she said. She then angrily placed them on the desk with a bang.

After cautioning the lad I asked him where the items were from.

'Like I told mi mam, I stole them from the corner shop on Dundas Road yesterday afternoon,' he replied sheepishly; and then went on to say, 'I'm very sorry.'

At that point his mum burst into tears but managed to say, 'I've brought him up on my own, 'cos his dad left me and it's been hard.' She then paused, then said, 'I've instilled it into him not to do anything daft or it will spoil his chance of a job.' She paused again. 'He needs to be taught a lesson so I told him I was taking him to the police station where he would be locked up.'

It was every parent's nightmare, teaching the kids the difference between right and wrong. The young lad, who was only sixteen, needed a wake-up call and his mum needed some practical help as well; she was beside herself with worry.

'Follow me,' I said with a stern voice and I took them both back downstairs.

'Can I have the keys to the prison cells please sergeant?' I asked and the sergeant handed them over.

The lad looked terrified as I opened the door and took both of them inside the Victorian cells. As I did so I winked at his mum and put my finger to my lips, signalling her to keep quiet. I pointed to the very low bed which was made of wooden planks, the same as the pillow, and said to the lad, 'This is where prisoners sleep after they have been to court, and there is no heating in the cell.'

The lad's face was a study as I let what I had said sink in, and then continued. 'Your mum must love you a lot, bringing you to the police station in the middle of the night. Stealing is a crime and not to be recommended to someone who is looking for a job. It would also mean a court appearance, resulting in a criminal record. I'm sure that you don't want to end up in prison sleeping on a bed like this, now do you?'

'No, sir,' he quickly replied as he, like us, shivered from the cold.

'Right, let's go back upstairs where it's warm and I will have a think,' I said in a serious voice; but I was inwardly chuckling to myself.

The lad's name was Alan and after I'd sat him and his mum down I looked at him and slowly started to speak. 'Right Alan, I can take you to court for stealing, where you will end up with a criminal record.' I paused and then continued. 'Or you can take these items back to the shop where you stole them from. Your mum must go with you so that I know that it's been done, and you also must apologize to the shopkeeper and your mother in the hope that they both forgive you. Okay? Now which one is it going to be Alan? I'm in a good mood tonight so I'm giving you the choice.'

I could see the look of relief on the lad's face, and it was obvious as I looked across at mum that she was more than happy at the way things were being handled.

'That last one, please sir,' Alan said.

'I thought you might say that, Alan, you didn't fancy a night in that cell did you?' and he shook his head. 'Right, come on then, grab your stuff and let's get you both home. It's late, and all sensible people should be in bed at this time of night.'

During the two-mile journey on the way to their home in Tinsley I gave the lad some more earache but also made sure that I complimented his mother on her actions, at the same time saying that if he ever did anything stupid in the future she must bring him to me where I would certainly lock him up. It turned out that he'd done it for a dare because his mate wanted some cigarettes – how stupid can you get? I've bumped into him six or seven times over the last forty-odd years, usually in a pub. He now owns a well-known electrical company in Rotherham and when he sees me it's always the same. 'Do you remember that night Mr Johnson and that cell that you showed me?' he'd say. Then he would laugh out loud and try to get me drunk. He would always finish up with the words, 'Thank you for what you did for me that night Mr Johnson. It certainly taught me a lesson.'

By this time it was about 2.30 in the morning and after lighting up a fag I set off back to the nick. Just as I got to Tinsley roundabout the car radio crackled into life. 'F' Division (road traffic) were in pursuit of a stolen car and for this reason their radio was left on 'open' channel. This meant that whoever was on patrol and with a radio, could hear their progress and the direction in which they were travelling in order that assistance would be readily available if anyone was in the area. I heard them mention that they were chasing the car down the Parkway and had then turned down Prince of Wales Road towards Darnall, about two miles from where I was; so I pulled up in a side street near to the Plumpers Hotel just in case they came my way. They could end up anywhere but I radioed my position in to control to say that I could cover the Tinsley roundabout area.

Listening to the radio told me that the car had left Prince of Wales Road and had turned back towards Handsworth and further away from my position so I lit another fag and waited. A few minutes later the car was back on Prince of Wales Road once more and was heading towards Attercliffe.

There was a few minutes radio silence after that, and then suddenly as I looked up Shepcote Lane I could see in the distance a car coming towards me at a very high speed; and behind it I could see a blue light flashing from the police car. With being in an unmarked police car I wasn't sure what I could do to stop him. He must have been doing 60 to 70 miles an hour but then, just before he got to the roundabout, he slowed right down and attempted to turn right into a side street opposite me. He slewed into the junction and collided with two parked vehicles which brought him to a stop.

As the following police car turned into the same road the driver of the stolen car somehow managed to reverse and rammed the car into the front of the police vehicle. At the same time the driver leapt out of the car and set off running in my direction. It had all happened in the blink of an eye. As I leapt out of the car he was running across some waste land with me in hot pursuit. I couldn't be sure but it looked as though he was limping and I was slowly catching him up. Just as I thought I'd got him, and was almost within reaching distance, he suddenly disappeared from right in front of me. A split second later there was a splash and too late I realized that Mr Car Thief had fallen into the canal – how sad I thought! It was impossible for me to stop and I was swearing like a good 'un, even before I, myself, ended up in the canal along with my best suit.

The Tinsley canal wasn't very wide or very deep for that matter, and when I surfaced I could see the man climbing out on the opposite bank a few feet away from me. At that point I scrambled out of the water and followed him as he ran up the steps of an iron footbridge which went over the railway line. I was closing on him once more when suddenly I heard a dog bark and then saw several torches flashing at the bottom of the steps on the other side of the bridge; there was now no escape for him. It was the police dog and handler and two other officers who had picked up on the radio messages and had come towards us from Attercliffe Common at the other side of the canal and near to Tinsley Wire Industries. At this point he was arrested by them, handcuffed and placed in a police car. If only I could have got my hands on him first. His actions had caused the two traffic lads to be injured and the maniac had ruined my best suit. I was livid – lock him up for life, I thought.

When Mr Car Thief was taken away the other policemen turned and saw that I was soaking wet, shivering and smelling like a sewer, and they cracked up laughing. The next two or three minutes of conversation between them and me are totally unprintable, but suffice it to say that in between laughing we also used words that are too delicate for me to use here.

Luckily for me one of the patrol cars had a plastic sheet in the boot of the car which they used when dealing with messy road traffic accidents. They were still laughing their heads off at the mess I was in when they put the plastic sheet on the back seat of the car with me sitting on it, and then thankfully drove me home to Thorpe Hesley about three miles away.

Poor Christine thought we'd got burglars as I noisily unlocked the front door and raced upstairs for the fastest shower that I'd ever had. Having told Christine what had happened before I had the shower saved some time as she'd organized me some clean clothes all ready for me as well as removing my police warrant card and other bits and bobs from the soggy suit. It was lovely to be nice and warm again and the lads dropped me back at my car which was where I'd left it earlier prior to the pursuit.

By the time I'd got back to the nick it was nearly 5am and I could have eaten a Skegness donkey, I was that hungry. When

I opened my packing up, or snap, it was made up of all the left overs from the two parties, including soggy egg sandwiches, bits of pork pie and sausage rolls. The only treats were two separate lumps of birthday cake covered in icing. It was obvious which piece of cake belonged to whom as one of the pieces was covered in candle fat obviously from the 100th birthday, whilst the other had none on at all.

A pint pot of tea later and a fag made me feel better at last but I was well and truly knackered from all the comings and goings; the sooner I got home the better. Just as I was getting ready to go home, at 6.50am the phone rang. What now, I thought. At the other end of the phone was Rick, my partner, 'What's up Rick?' I asked.

'I'm up at Spennymoor in County Durham. We've been to visit Doreen's family there.'

'Have you had a good weekend, mate?'

'Yes,' and he sounded stressed out of his brains, 'but the car engine's seized up and I need to get us and the car back to Sheffield. I'm not in the AA or RAC and I'm desperate.'

'What do you want me to do?' I asked. He replied with eight words: 'Come and tow me home pal, I'm desperate.'

'Bloody hell Rick, you must be a hundred miles away and I've been on nights,' I said and lit another fag at the thoughts of it. 'Okay, I'll borrow a tow rope from the police garage. I'm on my way – give me the address'; and then I wrote the address down that he gave me.

Back in those days the roads weren't nearly as good as they are today and I was dreading the long journey and just hoped that my old Ford Escort would be able to tow Rick's Ford Capri. At least the rope I'd borrowed from the police garage was a proper one and not flimsy. That was one thing I didn't have to worry about – the tow rope breaking.

Before leaving I'd phoned home to let Christine know what was happening so that she didn't worry, so when I'd finished work I made my way straight to the A1 and joined the other flotilla of cars and lorries heading north on the Monday morning. Just above Scotch Corner I joined the old B6275 Roman road which took me past what used to be the Roman town of Piercebridge, past Bishop Auckland and then joined the A688 to Spennymoor. Two and a half hours later I was treated to a pint pot of tea and a bacon and egg sandwich for which I was more than grateful. Rick was one of the best mates, as well as a colleague, that anybody could ever wish for and he would have done exactly the same for me without question.

The thoughts of the journey back worried us both, we needed to use the A1 to get us back home and it was illegal to tow a vehicle more than one junction but we had no option but to chance it. Rick had already made a sign for the back of his car which said 'ON TOW' so he fastened the sign on. Rick steered his car and Doreen was with me in my car as we set off south.

Luckily for us none of the return journey home was through hilly country which would have put a real strain on my old Escort. I was whacked before I'd even set off back and certainly didn't relish the idea. The journey back seemed to take forever and we kept pulling on and off the A1, stopping for a fag break and some fresh air at the occasional service station. The concentration level was intense but eventually, and after several hours we managed to get Rick and Doreen to their house in Sheffield.

Wow! First things first and Doreen put the kettle on while we unhitched the tow rope. Both Rick and I, although knackered, were both elated at what we'd achieved and like a pair of young lads we put our arms around each other and gave each other a hug.

'F......... hell!' screamed Rick, as he dropped to his knees on the floor.

The poor man was writhing about on the floor in agony.

'What's up Rick, what's up, what's the matter?' I said as Doreen tried to calm him down. I was so worried. What the hell was wrong? Poor old Rick could hardly get his breath and every time he breathed he winced in pain, holding his side.

It didn't sound like a heart attack to me but Doreen rang for an ambulance just in case. The emergency vehicle must have been nearby because it was with us within five minutes. It transpired that when we'd hugged each other, and not knowing my own strength, I'd unfortunately cracked Rick three ribs which is why he was struggling to breathe, poor lad. It was obviously an accident; and I wouldn't have knowingly hurt my mate for the world, but this didn't stop me feeling terrible – poor Rick! A broken down car and now three broken ribs to go with it, what a carry on!

He was later strapped up but unfortunately he was off work for a week or two.

By the time I got home it was about 4pm and I was absolutely drained – what a night and what a day! As I went to bed I realized that I had to be back at work in another seven hours – what would that shift bring, we never knew.

The next time I saw Rick we both had a laugh and I apologized and afterwards cheekily explained that I was 'only having a crack'. His reply is best forgotten!

Footnote: Unfortunately Rick and his wife Doreen both passed away at an early age. You couldn't wish for better friends; and Christine and I and all our family really miss them. We had some wonderful holidays and happy times together.

CHAPTER 14

What a Day Mi Owd Fruit!

The Sheffield Wholesale Market was alive with people and vehicles rushing around in all directions. Everyone was there, trying to buy their produce in the form of fish, flowers and vegetables as fast as they could in order to get them back to their own shops before opening time. It was always the same in the market between about 5am and 8am.

I started work at 7am and shortly after I received a phone call asking me to visit a large wholesale fruit and vegetable business within the Market, regarding a theft. At that time the manager, as far as my memory allows, was a grand lad called Paul and I used to call in every now and then; and I also used to bump into him from time to time at the Wholesale Fish Market when I'd call in for a nice piece of fresh fish or a crab for dinner.

Paul always got his priorities right and within minutes of my arrival I was presented with a mug of tea and a big bunch of bananas which he knew I loved. He was busy with a customer and as I supped my tea I made a little wager with myself and decided it would be one box as usual – or maybe two. The amount of stock which a wholesale fruit and veg dealer handled was enormous and was delivered on lorries from all over Britain on a 24-hour basis when it would be checked and signed for by the night watchman against what was on the delivery note. There were pallets stacked high with boxes of produce of all sorts of fruit and veg.

The small shopkeeper would buy one or two boxes of this, that or the other, whilst the big boys, who owned several outlets, might buy a pallet-full of each item; I don't know how they managed to keep track of everything and there were forklift trucks flying everywhere.

As I looked at all the people mingling about outside I spotted Sarah from the café who was buying fruit and veg ready for when the café opened; and I suddenly remembered that the last time I saw her was a couple of weeks ago; and she said that she wanted to see me about something or other. I gave her a wave and said that I would nip in to see her later on.

It was good timing and Paul came to talk to me, and I mischievously asked, 'One or two?'

'One,' he replied and frowned, 'but it's one f........ pallet full not one box – oh and guess what's in the boxes? Only f........ pineapples, our most expensive fruit.'

'I didn't know you sold pineapples, Paul, and it's not often you see them for sale,' I said.

'No, 'cos they're that bloody expensive – and hard to get hold of.'

'When did they arrive in the Market, Paul?'

'They and the delivery note were already here when I arrived at five this morning,' he replied, 'you know how busy we get and there's so much produce to keep an eye on. We're always on the lookout for some bastard nicking an odd box of apples or carrots – we're used to losing a box or two now and again as you know, but with a pallet full it's weird because you're not thinking about it being stolen; and I didn't realize that it was missing until about 7am which is when I rung you lads. It's not just the value of it, but how am I going to replace the pineapples; it's a special order for a stately home in Derbyshire who have organized a Calypso-themed party with several steel bands taking part over the weekend.' And he scratched his head in exasperation – and so did I as I took a statement off him and wondered where to begin.

Having driven round the market complex, checking out the other wholesale grocers to see what they were selling, I could see that there were no pineapples for sale so I left the market. Time to think over a pot of tea and a bacon and tomato sandwich, so I called in to see Sarah at her café. Sarah was a lovely lady of about 45 to 50 years of age and she looked most upset.

I used to use the café fairly often when I was on the beat and enjoyed chatting with Sarah and her Asian partner who she nicknamed 'Sam'. They were both very nice people and I got on with them really well. Eighteen months prior to this and before I went into CID Sarah seemed to be worried and one day I asked her what the problem was. It turned out that she was worried about Sam and the fact that he was getting involved too much with his brother who also ran a café; but at that point she wouldn't say anything else. Over a period of two or three months when Sam wasn't about, Sarah confided in me that Sam's brother was importing illegal immigrants into the country (something that was unheard of in the 1960s) and he was wanting Sam to get involved in doing some driving work for him; but Sam didn't want to know.

I knew his brother's café, which was in a busy part of our Division, and he owned a large transit-type van with an extended roof space, made of, I think, fibreglass. I can still remember the registration number today. Apparently Sam's brother used to drive down to Dover and pick up several illegal immigrants at a time and secrete them in the van. What happened when they got back to Sheffield, she didn't know. At one point Sam had been coerced into doing an illegal run for his brother and he was upset and worried that he had done so, but didn't know what to do as he was frightened of his brother who was a violent and evil man.

I reported the matter to a detective sergeant and, in turn, I was then asked to fill in a full and comprehensive report for a senior detective officer telling him how I knew what was happening and who had told me. A few weeks later I was told by the detective sergeant that the van had been pulled up on its journey back from Dover and inside were fruit machines, or one-armed bandits, which had been brought over from France; and that the information about the illegal immigrants was nonsense. There was nothing more that I could do, but it all seemed wrong to me and I wished that I hadn't naively told the senior officer where I'd got the information from. I didn't for one minute believe that the van had been checked out or that the information I'd been given was wrong.

Since I'd been told to go into CID I hadn't had many opportunities to go in to see Sarah and Sam as I used to do when working the beat. So I was determined to call in and see her and have a bacon and egg sandwich at the same time.

When I went into the café I could see that Sarah was worried about something and asked her to bring me up to date. Apparently Sam was spending more and more time with his brother, but under duress, and whenever she spoke to him about it, he clammed up, except to say that he was frightened of his brother. On one occasion during the night she'd heard him talking to himself in his sleep about drugs and pick-up points which worried her sick, as he was sometimes away for two to three days at a time.

Then she told me that she hadn't seen Sam for over a week and she was sick with worry. Having finished my breakfast I left the café and went back to the office after telling Sarah to keep me informed if anything cropped up and I would call and see her again soon.

By the time I'd got back to the office it would be about 9am, so I mashed a pot of tea – as all good detectives do, grabbed an ash tray and found an empty desk as Detective Sergeant Len Buxton was interviewing someone at mine.

Pineapples, pineapples, pineapples – I couldn't get the bloody word out of my head. Today they aren't unusual and you can buy them almost anywhere, but forty-odd years ago fresh pineapples were far from common and you had to make do with tinned pineapples to put on your gammon steak or cocktail sticks. I quickly telephoned several different green grocers I knew which were scattered around different parts of the city, including my old landlady's son George ('Jud') Proctor, who was a bit of a rogue. Not one of them had seen, never mind been offered any pineapples for several weeks. For that reason, logic told me that the stolen pineapples were no longer in Sheffield. So where do I go from here?

I read Paul's statement and realized that they had been stolen sometime between 5am and 7am, so how had they been stolen without anybody noticing? A pallet is far too big to be manhandled and would need a forklift truck to move it. Looking at the delivery note told me that the goods had been delivered to the Sheffield Market by a fruit wholesaler situated in Bradford, some forty miles away, so I telephoned them.

Apparently they were also importers of unusual fruits, such as pineapples, and regularly delivered goods to other wholesalers around the country including Sheffield. I explained to the lady over the phone what had happened and where it had happened and she was most surprised; and once more I thought where do we go from here?

About fifteen minutes later I received a telephone call from the owner of the company that I had just spoken to and he sounded fairly nervous. 'How can I help you?' I asked, 'you've obviously rung me for a reason.'

'Hi, my name is Dave and I'm the owner of the Wholesale Import Company that you rang this morning. The girl in the office has just told me what's happened with the pineapples that we would have delivered to Sheffield at around 4.30am today. What I am about to say is a very delicate matter for me and something that I have been putting off for a little while in the hope that I was wrong. Will you guarantee that I am talking in confidence to you if what I am going to tell you doesn't help?'

'You have my word, yes,' I answered; and I was intrigued as to what he was going to say.

'I think I might be employing a dodgy driver and the word on the street is that he and a mate of his have set up a small business similar to our own and are selling stuff cheaper than we are. We have had one or two complaints in the Bradford and Leeds areas where stuff has gone missing after having been dropped off by the driver. This is the first enquiry I've had from Sheffield and it seems too coincidental that it is the same driver who has delivered the goods to the other premises from where we have had the complaints.

'Wow, that is interesting. Do you, by any chance, know where these other premises are?'

'I'm not one hundred per cent certain because all the complaints have come in over the last month so I haven't had the chance to check.'

'You know the other complaints you've had, have the items been left on pallets?'

'No,' he said, 'just sometimes two, three or four boxes of fruit – maybe oranges, apples or whatever. Usually seasonal fruits but occasionally an odd box of exotic fruit.'

I asked for the address that they may possibly be operating from and I asked him to stay in the office while I made more enquiries, which he agreed to do.

At that point I lit another fag and thought how interesting this could turn out to be. I realized that this might be a hot lead and that if, in fact, there was a connection to our job I would have to act fast. By this time it would be about 10am when I phoned the police in Bradford and asked to speak to a detective sergeant at headquarters. I outlined the situation to him and said that I knew that they were very busy but I wondered whether they could help me out. I gave him the possible address that I had been given and as far as I can remember the detective sergeant told me that the address I'd given him was in the Manningham district of Bradford; and he put me through to the Division that covered that area.

Once more I explained the situation to another detective sergeant and told him that, although it was only a possibility, if the premises could be discreetly observed, and if we were correct in our thinking, then it would clear up our crime and, from the sound of it, some crimes that they themselves were dealing with.

I further explained to him that there was a possibility of catching the culprits in possession of our stolen property – the pineapples; and if the information could be acted upon quickly it would greatly improve our chances of an arrest. Thankfully, he said that he had read the situation and I should leave it with him and he and one of the lads would go and have a sniff around. Brilliant, I thought, that'll do for me so I mashed a pot of tea, ate two of my bananas and then lit up another fag.

After that I was on edge, not so much because it would be a decent job to prove but because of poor Paul's predicament as well as that of the stately home and its concert. I tried to do some paper work but my heart wasn't in it so after a while I packed it in. Three-quarters of an hour later the phone went, yet again. It was the detective sergeant from Bradford.

'I think you might be right mate. It looks like a small concern with boxes here, there and everywhere but there is what looks like a new pallet with a lot of boxes on. I can't see into the boxes and don't want to blow our cover and spoil the job. If you and your mate can get over here as fast as possible before they're sold then me and my mate will keep observations until you arrive. Is that a deal?'

'You bet it's a bloody deal mate, thank you very much.'

Rick explained to Detective Inspector Hepworth what was what, while I telephoned Dave, the owner of the importers in Bradford asking him to meet up with us. We agreed on a place to meet in roughly an hour's time and with that Rick and I were on our way.

By the time we met up with the importer it was about 1.15pm and he guided us to where we'd arranged to meet the other detectives, a small distance away from the premises concerned. Fingers crossed.

The Bradford detectives pointed further down the road to a small set of premises whose wooden front doors were wide open; and knowing that anybody in them would neither recognize me or the CID car, we decided to drive past without Rick or me looking inside; but instead to let Dave, who was in the back seat, have a discreet look as we drove past. A few minutes later as we were passing the premises I heard a broad Bradford voice shout, 'The f........ bastards, that's definitely our stuff and on that pallet are your pineapples, no ifs or buts. I know because I loaded them onto the lorry myself yesterday evening.'

We parked the car up and the three of us walked into the premises where a man was seen moving some boxes. The look on his face was amazing as I first of all explained to him who Rick and I were (Sheffield detectives) and then Dave (the owner of the wholesale importers). He had a face that even his pet dog wouldn't lick and was visibly shocked when Dave told him about the pineapples that were missing from Sheffield Wholesale Market.

Dave was over the moon just like we were, and I couldn't wait to ring Paul to tell him what had happened; but that would just have to wait as the market would now be closed. We arrested the bloke in the premises and took him back to Bradford Divisional Headquarters which was a beautiful old building, and interviewed him where he readily admitted to handling stolen property; and at the same time he grassed up the driver who had stolen the pineapples.

It was obvious that a few boxes were missing from the pile but according to Dave there were at least three-quarters of the pallet full still there. What a gentleman – Dave was mortified that the pineapples had been stolen in the first place and especially as they were a special order. Knowing that Paul wouldn't have been able to replace them because of their scarcity he offered to take them to Sheffield during the night so that Paul and the stately home were not let down. Brilliant mate, thank you, I thought.

The two blokes were then interviewed by the Bradford detectives and admitted the theft of the boxes that Dave had complained about – which had gone missing from Leeds and Bradford – thus clearing up some of the crimes in their area just as we'd hoped.

For that reason it was decided to charge the blokes there, keep them at Bradford and ultimately for them to attend the court in Bradford. If they had only admitted to stealing the pineapples and not the other jobs then we would have had to take them back to Sheffield where they had committed the offence; and then charge them and take them to court there. They must have later admitted to all the offences in the Bradford court but because Rick and I were never called to give evidence. I don't know what happened to them; and what's more, I didn't really care – job done.

CHAPTER 15

A Fighting Chance

I've never been an early riser and I am never up before the alarm tells me to. Christine is the opposite of me and is always up at about 5.30am. I'm sure there'll be someone out there, it maybe you, who will put me straight, but I put it down to working a three-shift system and my body clock being all over the place – or is it just idleness?

The previous day had been a long one with yet another five-and-a-half hours of unpaid overtime work. Within three hours of me getting home I was in bed again and looking forward to going to work the following day. A few years before I got married I, unbelievably, overslept and was late getting to work for the night shift, which started at 11pm. I was fined £1 for neglect of duty and the other lads never let me live it down.

At 5.30am I heard a ringing and a clattering noise which would have even woken the dead. Leaping out of bed, I removed the alarm clock from within the metal saucepan and switched it off. The old Superintendent who had fined me £1 for being late a few years ago, was right when he advised me to put the alarm clock into a metal saucepan – it never failed.

Christine was already downstairs with a couple of slices of toast and a mug of tea waiting for me – what a lucky man I was, and still am today, Christine has always been a cracker. After a quick kiss I grabbed my snap and fags and I was off down the M1. Unusually for me I couldn't wait to get to work.

Arriving at work earlier than normal I grabbed the CID car keys and I was off, back to the Wholesale Market to see Paul. It had been too late to contact him the day before and I'd have given anything to have been in the market at about 5am when he would have, most likely, seen his pallet of pineapples – what must he have thought? He wouldn't have had a clue as to how they got there and I was hoping to have a bit of fun with him at his expense.

As I sidled down the outside of Paul's warehouse I could see the pallet of pineapples near to where I was and I could also see another delivery note with a letter stapled to it. As I retrieved the note from one of the boxes I read the letter of apology from Dave in Bradford and I then slipped it into my pocket. Paul was busy selling produce so I sneaked round to the front of the building where I could see him. Perfect – he was now facing me and his pallet of pineapples were behind him.

I had to get the timing right and be the first one to speak, so I waited until he'd finished serving.

'Morning, Paul – no good news about your pineapples mate, they could be anywhere by now,' I shouted over the customers' heads. As he looked up at me his mouth dropped open and his face was a picture. He slowly turned and pointed to the pallet with his right arm outstretched and a puzzled look on his face. How I didn't burst out laughing I'll never know as he slowly said, 'They're there, Martyn' and his mouth dropped open again.

'Bloody hell Paul,' I shouted, 'are you telling me that you misplaced them after all and that I've been running round like a blue-arsed fly trying to find them?'

'No, they were definitely stolen yesterday,' he said exasperatedly, 'but now, somehow, they're back here, but with four or five boxes missing.' And he shook his head, saying, 'I think I'm going f...... crackers.'

The look on his face was truly amazing and it was a shame to spoil the fun, but I couldn't contain myself any longer and, as I handed him the delivery note and the letter, I burst out laughing. I led him into his office in a bemused state; and I put the kettle on and mashed as he, alternately kept scratching his head, re-reading the letter and shaking his head in bewilderment. We both sat down and lit a fag and I then talked him through the previous day's events and his eyes opened wide in amazement. I also explained to him that by the time Rick and myself had finished the enquiry the market was closed so I couldn't let him know the results; and the fact that his produce had been recovered and better still, returned to him during the night.

'Martyn, that is quite simply amazing and you and your mate have done a brilliant job, but if that bent bastard of a driver dropped the pineapples here in the beginning, how did you end up recovering them in Bradford – how did they get there?' Paul asked in a perplexed manner.

'Easy Paul – after dropping off your pallet the driver went to have his breakfast at the market café. When he'd finished he saw that you were busy with customers so he stopped one of the passing forklift truck lads and explained that he had accidently dropped the pallet off at the wrong shop instead of a shop further across the market. The lad on the forklift truck fell for it and in less than a minute the pallet was back on his lorry. The innocent forklift driver went about his other duties and our lorry driver then left the market and dropped your stuff off with his mate in Bradford.'

'The crafty bastard, I can't believe it,' Paul said.

'It was the same in Leeds and Bradford, our lorry driver would have dropped off boxes of produce outside shops in the early morning and then his mate, who knew his route, would follow in a van and nick the stuff before the shops were open for business – as simple as that Paul.'

Needless to say both Paul and I were chuffed to bits at the outcome; we'd recovered and organized for the return of most of Paul's stolen goods which was enough for him to complete his 'special' order to the 'big house' in Derbyshire in time for the Calypso-themed event.

Without the willing help and prompt action by the Bradford Police Force we wouldn't have stood a chance in detecting the crime; and they were happy because it had cleared several jobs up for them and the Leeds Police Force. Everyone was happy and a few days later Rick and I received a nice letter of thanks from Brian in Bradford. Even Christine was pleased as Paul presented Rick and me with a parcel of fruit and veg including a fresh pineapple each – delicious – thanks Paul. If only all the crimes that we had to detect were solved as quickly as that it would have made our lives a lot easier.

I was looking forward to Saturday when some of our uniformed lads, as well as several detectives, had been seconded to work with the Doncaster Police Force which was about fifteen miles away. We were being sent to help out at one of the biggest sporting events of the year – the St Leger horse race.

The first St Leger horse race was run in 1776, which must make it one of the oldest horse races in the country and is certainly the first of the five classics. For several reasons it reminded me of when I was a kid growing up in Darfield. One of the founders of the race was the Marquis of Rockingham who lived in Wentworth Woodhouse, an enormous mansion in the village of Wentworth, where I now live. Both my mum and grandma remembered and had told me stories about Earl

Fitzwilliam, the then owner of Wentworth Woodhouse who would travel, with his family and guests, through Darfield on their way to the races in a cavalcade of open-topped cars. It wasn't their quickest route to the races but in the depression of the 1920s and the miners' strike, it meant that they avoided travelling through villages that were hostile towards them for being one of the richest families in the land. Their wealth was as a result of their ownership of vast amounts of land in the area which contained both iron and coal deposits.

Mum always used to say that they all knew when they had had a good day at the races, and she had vivid and happy memories of those times. The Fitzwilliams and their guests, which included His Highness The Aga Khan, would stay at the mansion during Race Week.

All the children in the village would gather together awaiting the return of the Fitzwilliams and their guests from the races. If they'd had a poor day they used to throw handfuls of the famous Doncaster Butter Scotch to the waiting children, but if they'd had a good day at the races not only would they throw the Butter Scotch, they would also throw handfuls of shiny pennies, halfpennies and occasionally silver three-penny bits and sixpences as they were cheered on their way by the children.

My other memory of the races happened when I was about eight years of age. The local British Legion Club, of which my dad was a member, had organized a bus trip to the races at Doncaster and, along with my mum, dad and sister we went on the trip. I didn't know what 'going to the races' meant but when I saw the huge fair ground and all the different stalls I remember being really excited. There were thousands of people like us there and either mum or dad held our hands all day to stop us getting lost. Probably like my dad I've never been into horses or gambling and, as far as I am aware, we never saw a race that day, but what I did see is something that I'll never forget and along with my sister I was absolutely terrified.

As we were walking through the crowds I saw something coming towards me but I didn't know what it was and at the same time I heard the shout of 'I've gotta horse' but as I looked around me I couldn't see one. What I did see was a giant black man – the first one that I'd ever seen. He was wearing a really weird costume of massive baggy trousers and a really large and very colourful jacket and waistcoat. But on his head was a huge headdress full of what I now know to be different coloured ostrich feathers. I was absolutely terrified and clung to dad. Both mum and dad tried to calm us down and as the man bent down he was smiling and waving to us but kept shouting, 'I gotta horse', and at the same time he was waving paper envelopes about in his hand.

Mum and dad were both laughing and told me that he was a very nice man and not to be frightened. At that point my dad told me that this giant black man was in fact a Zulu Prince from Africa. I knew that elephants and giraffes lived in Africa as well as lions and tigers but I didn't realize until then that people also lived in Africa.

Over the next few years we went on the same trip on several occasions and the man was always there laughing and smiling and dressed in colourful clothes and waving paper envelopes about and shouting 'I gotta horse'. It was sixty-five years ago but I can still remember it as if it was yesterday. His name was Prince Monolulu and he was, in fact, a celebrity tipster; and I later found out that he went round all the famous racecourses in England selling tips, which apparently he was very, very good at.

On my arrival at the course today I looked around me to see that nothing much had changed. There were still many thousands of people milling around as well as modern fun fairs and stalls. I was expecting to hear the words 'I gotta horse' and to see that amazing man who had at first frightened me as a nipper but that now I had fond memories of – Prince Monolulu but he was nowhere to be seen except in my memory.

What was there however were plenty of British and foreign dignitaries in the form of lords, ladies, sirs and I was also told, royalty. The other thing that I was told was that it was believed that several 'dippers' or pick-pockets were also in attendance which is why we were there. The year before this I'd managed to catch one of Fagin's gang at the Finningley Air Show (see *What's Tha up To This Time?*) but it was more by good luck than good judgement. These lads are proper professionals and not easy to spot never mind catch. I wore the same clothes this year as I did at Finningley in the hope that it would bring me luck and I also placed my own wallet inside my shirt and wedged into the waistband of my jeans. I didn't want anyone nicking it as it contained my police warrant card, two pound notes and a skew-whiff picture of 'daddy' drawn by my little lad Richard, something that I still have today.

There was a real buzz about the place and I think Lester Piggott had won the three previous St Leger races. As I stood and watched the 'on-course' bookies I could see that they were all doing a brisk trade with money going backwards and forwards between them and the lucky punters who had won. As the races were being won, including the St Leger itself, I placed myself near to the winning post, but behind the large crowds which were surging forwards to get a better view of the horses as they passed by. It was unbelievable to see men stretching forward and exposing their wallets sticking out of their back trousers pockets for all to see. I was sure I was going to catch at least one dipper today; and my eyes were darting from left to right like windscreen wipers as I watched the crowd at every race; but unfortunately I never got a 'sniff' of one, which really pissed me off.

You can't win 'em all, and I'd won one last year so maybe next year I'd be lucky again I'd hoped. Out of about sixty complaints of thefts received during the day there were only two dippers caught – I told you that they were clever.

Our day wasn't over yet and we were asked to go across from the track and around the corner to a large pub and assist if needed; 'assist if needed – needed to what' I thought, 'if it's to sup a pint in the pub that'll suit me fine;' but I realized that I wouldn't be that lucky.

As I trudged across the road I spotted a uniformed Doncaster bobby who looked to be an old timer, walking in the same direction as me. It was Mick Holgate who I had mated up with at training school in 1962, so after exchanging pleasantries I asked him what all the fuss was about.

'Each year a number of the gypsy and traveller communities turn up in Doncaster for Race Week, just like everyone else'; and he pointed across the road to where I could see several traditional gypsy caravans and lots of modern ones. Their horses were tethered nearby. 'Historically they have been coming here since the race began. The gypsies love their horses,' Mick explained.

'How does that affect us, Mick, what are we on standby for?' I asked.

'Some of the gypsy families have a male member of the family who is good at fighting and when they get together, like as now, they all arrange to meet up together with their respective 'champion'. Each fighter buys a new suit and puts a hundred pounds into a kitty; and then they fight. It is 'winner take all';

and the winner is the man who is still standing and still with most of his suit intact.' Mick continued: 'Obviously they are going to get injured but the injuries are not as serious as you would expect and certainly not life threatening.'

'You must be joking, they've got to be mad,' I said in amazement.

'It's a tradition that they've kept up over the years and it's their way of sorting out family feuds. In fairness to them, they don't mean any harm to anyone other than themselves. They police the fight themselves and that's why we are on standby duties just in case. Each year they arrange it with the landlord of the pub, who removes all the moveable furniture, and whatever damages are done they, themselves pay for and as far as I am aware they have never failed to do so yet.'

'So it's like an illegal boxing match but indoors?'

'That's it, yes,' Mick replied.

'I can't believe it,' I said. 'How weird.'

On our arrival at the pub I was surprised to see, as we stood outside, several smartly dressed young men of various ages but all looked as mean as mustard and you could tell that they were fighters all right, make no mistake about it: they were toughies.

It was a low-key gathering and we watched from a distance. At an appointed time all the blokes finished their beer and went into the pub. There were probably about a dozen to fifteen men and presumably the fight must have started within the pub, as after a couple of minutes a chap came out wearing only half a suit jacket and with blood pouring from his nose. A few minutes later out came another with a torn shirt, no sleeve in his jacket and holding one arm with the other; and he appeared to have a broken arm.

One by one and over a period of time they all came out in various stages of undress and evident injuries. It was one of the weirdest things I have ever seen. You could hear shouting in the pub and people crashing about, until eventually a chap came out, still with his trousers on, all of his jacket on apart from one lapel, that had been ripped off, blood all over his white shirt, coming from what looked like a broken nose; and both his eyes were swollen up. He'd obviously been announced the winner and great cheers went up amongst the crowd of travellers who were standing outside. Some of the men were limping or holding broken fingers, etcetera; but as Mick had said earlier, it was their way of sorting out family squabbles and feuds in their own way.

We were never called to the building so I don't know what it was like inside but it must have been okay. They all shook hands and went back inside and that was the end of that. I couldn't stop shaking my head in amazement and I couldn't believe what I'd just seen. I couldn't stop laughing.

That incident took place over forty years ago, but whether it still takes place now I don't know.

CHAPTER 16

What a Palaver

My colleague John, just like Rick, was a great bloke to work with and also a great character. We'd had a tip off that a woman called Susan, who lived somewhere in the Pitsmoor area of the city, had been trying to sell some stolen jewellery to several of the people in our Division who ran swap/second-hand shops. As a police force we issued weekly notices listing a description of the items stolen that week to these types of shops and also to pawnbrokers. This was done in the hope that if ever any of the shops were offered the stolen goods – as in fact had happened in this instance – then they would be required to let us know. If they didn't let us know and had then bought the stolen goods after reading the notices, we would be able to charge them with handling stolen property. The tip off had been passed to John and it was now up to him to make further enquiries. Who was 'Susan'? We didn't know, but John said that he knew a girl who lived in the Pitsmoor area and he was sure that it would be her.

'John, there must be loads of girls in that area called Susan, how can you be so sure it's her?' I asked.

'She's got blonde hair and glasses just like the people in the shops described her – that's why,' said John.

'Has this Susan that you know been in bother before, John?'

'I would imagine so, looking at her,' said John, 'let's see if there's a mug shot of her in the Rogues Gallery files.'

John couldn't spot her and kept going on about how he thought it would still be her.

'John, just because this woman told one of the shop owners that her name was Susan and that she lived in Pitsmoor doesn't mean owt, mate. She'd be telling lies to avoid detection anyway.'

John would have none of it and said, 'I'm telling you, I still think it's her. Come on, I think I can remember where she lived and its a few doors away from my auntie's house on Abbeyfield Road.' By this time it would be about seven on a Friday night and the roads were fairly quiet as we set off to find John's mystery woman. As I was driving John explained to me that he used to see her when he visited his auntie's house who died about four years ago. He hadn't seen her since then but he always thought that she was shifty looking and up to no good.

We pulled up to where we could see the house concerned, a short distance away, and we waited for, maybe, half an hour. If John had something in his head, and being senior to me, then it was always worth a shot – I'd worked with him before and he had an uncanny habit of being right.

A few minutes later the number 75 bus pulled up at the bus stop across the road and four people got off: a lad on his own, a lady with a child; and unbelievably, a blonde-haired young woman with glasses on aged about twenty-five. I was inwardly chuckling to myself as John jumped out of the car and the expression 'a bull in a china shop' came into mind.

As I followed John across the road I could see that the woman was carrying a large holdall and that she looked smartly dressed in flat black shoes, black stockings, a navy blue skirt and a purple padded jacket. As she got near to us John took out his warrant card, held it towards her and said in a rough voice, 'Police – I am Detective Constable Longbottom and this is Detective Constable Johnson; and we're making enquiries about some stolen jewellery.'

Before John could continue the woman gave us a lovely smile and said, 'Wow, that's exciting, I'd love to help you.'

'That's what we were hoping for,' said John in a stern voice, 'because we know that you can help us.' At that point a look of real disappointment and a frown came across the woman's face and then she said, 'I'm very sorry but I can't help you right now, I'm just coming home after my second month of training at the police college.'

As John and I looked at each other in sheer amazement I could see that John's mouth was opening and closing and he didn't know what to say; and so I said to the girl apologetically, 'That's practical lesson number one for you, now you know how to introduce yourself to a potential prisoner. We don't really need any help but John had heard that you'd joined the police force and wanted to help you out.'

At that point she was all thanks and once more I had to speak before John further put his foot in it. 'When you've finished your police training we'll see if we can arrange for you to work down the 'Cliffe with us, you'll find it really interesting.'

'That would be brilliant, thanks,' she said, 'I'd love that.'

With that I grabbed John and took him back to the car out of harm's way where once inside I exploded into laughter. Being John he couldn't see the funny side of it at first but then grudgingly said, 'Well it could have been her, but she didn't look like that the last time I saw her.'

'Come on John, let's go for a pint,' I said and I just could not stop laughing.

We weren't a million miles from Mucky Mary's and ten minutes later in we walked to the usual sound of 'ONE, TWO, THREE, CID'. There was hardly anybody in the place so I asked Cecil for two halves and three for the lads in the snug ;and said, 'John will gladly pay tonight lads,' which he did and they all raised their glasses and shouted, 'THANKS SWEETIE,' to him.

We were having our usual banter with the lads in the snug and John just kept slowly shaking his head and then bursting into laughter thinking about probably one of the biggest clangers of his life. In the next breath the cheeky bugger changed his tune and said, 'Bloody hell, she's changed since I last saw her but at least I still recognized her and I'll tell you what Martyn, I'll bet she'll make a damned good policewoman.' As he said that I nearly spilt my beer and said, 'You've got more faces than the Town Hall clock John.' And we both set off laughing again, I just could not believe what I had witnessed – the dozy pillock.

A few minutes later and now on our second half I heard someone shouting from the other room, which I thought was empty. Poking my head around the corner revealed Big Basil, a regular visitor to the pub and once more I set off laughing. Mary's pub had it all or so I thought until I saw Big Basil. He was the only person in the room and with a pint in one hand he was slowly jigging away to the music coming from the juke-box. He'd obviously had a few to drink and was in a world of his own so I turned back to the bar. A minute or two later I could hear loud talking again and this time it was John who turned to look. He was just having a swig from his glass, when he pointed into the other room and at the same time he sprayed his beer all over. I wondered what was going off and turned to see for myself what the fuss was all about.

There in the middle of the room was Big Basil who was singing in a calypso way.

'Whoo wantsa link o' black puddin'?' He was obviously drunk and his trousers were undone, and there lying on the table top for all to see, was the reason why he was called 'Big Basil'.

'Basil. What's up with you?' I said, 'put that bloody big thing away.'

'I fed up Mr Johnson,' Basil replied, 'Friday night and I gotta no business – no business, no money. I fed up.'

Mary must have heard the lads in the snug laughing, as well as us and she came down to see what the commotion was about and she laughed when we told her what was what.

The saying 'it takes all sorts' came to mind. Some of the lads in the snug were male prostitutes looking for other men whilst some of the girls who used the other room where Basil was now on his own were female prostitutes looking for men; and I think it was the only time I'd been in there when none of the girls were in. They were obviously out there doing a brisk trade. Basil was different, he was a tall good-looking guy and he was a prostitute who sold himself, for the night, to rich women; and I had to wonder whether these same women bought by the inch or the foot! I'm glad my missus didn't see it or I'd have got the sack.

What a place and what characters, like no other pub I'd ever been into before or since.

Time to get back to the nick to see what was happening, if anything. I should have known better, let's face it Friday night, pay-day and the pubs were open – if that wasn't a recipe for trouble down the 'Cliffe I don't know what was.

As we drove up Burngreave and then down Barnsley Road towards Fir Vale I saw a blue light flashing behind me so I slowed down to let it pass assuming that it was an ambulance on its way to the nearby Northern General Hospital. As it drew alongside, I could see that it was, in fact, the Black Maria or police van. At the same time the car radio crackled into life: 'Any mobile in the vicinity of the Pheasant public house at Sheffield Lane Top attend immediately. A fight is taking place and two officers have been injured.'

Although we were detectives, not attending the incident was NOT an option; and with that I dropped down from fourth gear to third to gain more power, and we were off. The Black Maria with the blue light flashing slowly made its way through the red light at the traffic system at the bottom of Page Hall Road but with us being in an unmarked police car and with no flashing lights meant that we daren't chance it for obvious reasons. Green means go, which is just what I did when the lights changed. First, second and then third gear as I sped up the hill towards the incident a mile away.

Wow, what a sight, it looked like a riot. The Black Maria, four or five Panda cars, which I knew would only have one officer in each car, and a police dog and handler. I could also see a road traffic police car and an ambulance near to two crashed cars in the middle of the crossroads.

There must have been about thirty or forty men fighting and some were wrestling with each other and rolling about in the road.

Where the hell do you begin? As I was the driver, John was out of the car first and I saw him get hold of a bloke who was just going to hit someone over the head with a beer bottle. John hit the bloke and, as he fell to the floor, he managed to get the bottle off him. At the same time another chap hit John over the head with a metal dustbin lid and he went down as well. I grabbed the bloke who had clouted John and 'chinned him'. He was out for the count and I quickly spun round to look for John but couldn't see him – it was absolute bedlam and we were in the thick of it.

'John,' I shouted as loud as I could, 'where the hell are you?'

'Over here in the police van,' he weakly replied.

At that moment I felt someone grab my arms from behind and at the same time as I was dropping to my knees I leaned forward and pulled hard on his arms. He came over my head and shoulders and landed on the pavement in front of me with a thud. I bunched my fist and was just about to let him have one when I saw that it was a policeman who I didn't know. As he scrambled for his truncheon I realized what was happening and yelled, 'CID – there are two of us here.' And by this time I flashed my warrant card.

'Martyn tell him who I am!' It was John who was a few yards away in the back of the prison van, I could see that his arms were behind his back and then realized that he was handcuffed. What a palaver. The lads were from a different division – they didn't know us and we didn't know them and they had understandably thought that we were part of the mob.

As John was released from the 'cuffs I could see a three-inch gash on his scalp which was bleeding heavily and he looked really groggy. By now there were blue lights and bobbies everywhere in attendance from all over the city. Because of the extra men the situation was, more or less, under control and so I decided to take John to Casualty at the Northern General Hospital. There were four uniformed lads there already suffering from various injuries, including one with a broken arm, another with a dislocated shoulder and the other two with not so nice facial injuries having been kicked whilst on the floor. My own left eye felt sore and it was only later on when I went to the toilet and looked in the mirror that I could see a shiner on its way. It must have happened when I was sorting out the chap with the dustbin lid but at the time I oddly enough, never felt a thing. As well as bobbies being in casualty, there were also prisoners and non-prisoners with similar injuries to our own and consistent with having been in a brawl. Over the next half an hour a few more arrived as did another two policemen who were well-bloodied.

The poor doctors and nurses were run off their feet and when tempers flared up again between what now appeared to be two rival factions amongst the injured civilians, I had to get involved. I was the only one not waiting for treatment and for the sake of the doctors and nurses I found it necessary, on a couple of occasions, to intervene in order to stop a fight in the hospital itself. Over several hours the majority of people had been treated and most people like John, were free to leave the hospital.

Poor old John had to have several stitches in his head and he was also concussed and suffering serious headaches, so I took him straight home to Woodhouse, where he lived.

The doctor had instructed him to stay in a darkened room for a few days and he was off work for two weeks. It must have been about 4am when I got home and I went straight to bed. I was knackered but as I went through the night's events in my mind I could still see the look of amazement on John's face when he realized that Susan, his number-one-suspect, was in fact a trainee policewoman. It set me off chuckling to myself and then it turned into uncontrollable silent laughter, which made the bed bounce; and Christine woke up and switched on the bedside light. She wasn't amused at being woken up but then she saw my eye which by now had really swollen up and was almost closed. 'There's something wrong with you – a nasty black eye like that and you're in bed laughing like a drain.' She shook her head, switched off the light in a huff and then got back under the covers – I hadn't spoken a word – funny things women.

The following afternoon when I got to work I took some stick off the lads, which I expected with having a black eye.

'I see he's had some shut eye,' said one.

Another one from across the room said, 'We'll have to keep an eye open for him,' and so on – but of course I'd be making the same quips myself if it was them and not me.

I'd already phoned Mabel, John's wife, who told me that he was still in bed with the curtains closed and that his headaches were easing a little.

Although nowhere near headline material, the incident made the Sheffield newspaper: 'Several People Hurt in Skirmish', I seem to remember it said. I made enquiries and apparently it had all started when a stolen car had gone through the lights on red at the crossroads near the pub and it had then smashed into another car containing four rugby players on their way back from a match. Both cars were unable to be removed and the three lads in the stolen car ran into the Pheasant pub which turned out to be their local. The rugby lads, after phoning the police, went in after them and dragged two of them out and took them to the road patrol car which was just arriving at the scene. As the officers tried to arrest the local lads who had been driving the stolen car, a fight kicked off and their mates from the pub also joined in.

The two officers were head butted and knocked to the floor and the rugby lads were trying to stop them getting a good kicking. Some passers-by who saw what was happening also came to help. By now more policemen had arrived as well as the ambulance and, as the policemen were taken to hospital along with one of the rugby lads, the fighting flared up again; and in the end no one knew who was fighting who. That was the situation as John and I turned up in plain clothes, and pitched in to help – no wonder then why we both nearly got locked up.

People could have easily been killed that night but I'll bet that most of the people who got locked up ended up with a slap on the wrist.

A couple of weeks later John arrived back at work and, being a popular guy, everyone clapped him into the office. At that point Rick piped up, 'John, nice to see you back mate. Do you know the name of a lady from Pitsmoor who may handle stolen jewellery?' and we all laughed.

I thought it best to leave some empty space now for you to fill in the words of reply that you think John might have made – I daren't write them down.

CHAPTER 17

Good Cop - Bad Cop

What a glorious day – the sun was shining, the birds were singing and the weather forecast was brilliant. Just what we needed on my two days off. My old and battered Ford Escort was groaning under the weight of everything that my wife decided was necessary to take with us on our two-day break. I was sure she'd emptied the house.

I'll bet you lads will know what's coming next – twenty miles into the journey and just as we were crossing over the top of the beautiful Pennine hills and towards Manchester, Christine suddenly shouted, 'I've forgotten Richard's nappies and the tins of baby food, we'll have to go back!' My face must have looked like an angry wasp and the words that were passing through my mind are unprintable.

'If you think I'm going back for nappies and baby food, then you've got another thing coming, we'll buy some in Blackpool when we get there,' I said.

The next bit of the journey was in complete and stony silence apart from Richard crying because his bum needed changing. The smell was horrendous and, even though I had to open the car windows, by the time I found a chemist shop in Stalybridge I was 'as nazi as a crab's backside'.

I was lucky that back on my old beat in Sheffield was the Heinz food distribution centre on Coleford Road. I'd dealt with quite a few jobs there over the years and I often called in for a pot of tea. When Richard was born the staff very kindly saved me any slightly dented tins of baby food – what a bonus.

Nipping into the chemist shop, I asked for some nappies and enough tins of Heinz baby food to last the weekend. When they told me the price I gave the Barnsley war cry, 'How much?' I couldn't believe it, I was nearly skint and we hadn't even got to Blackpool.

Christine changed Richard's nappy and fed him and after that they both fell asleep. During the rest of the journey I was musing to myself about my cousin Walter Jackson who had been my Best Man at our wedding. He was the son of Uncle Jack. Jack had been a 'rough and ready' farmer in Barnsley all his life and Walter's three brothers (John, Peter and Jim) followed in his footsteps, were farmers themselves. Walter, though, went in a different direction; he was an expert on wines and gourmet food and was the manager of the Cooperative Wine Department in Barnsley and had managed to save enough money to use as a deposit on the purchase of 'The Royton', a small private hotel on Albert Road in Blackpool. Walter was a great guy and after he'd settled in he seemed to be doing all right and had invited us over to spend a free weekend with him.

On our arrival we had a beautiful meal, but in the kitchens downstairs away from the paying guests and before we went to bed, Walter told us that there was to be a special treat the following morning, which was Sunday, but he didn't tell us what it was. The following morning he gave us a light breakfast and then we walked on Blackpool front to what we were told was an Irish pub that was very much the 'in' place to go. It was beautiful inside, and to add to the atmosphere there was sawdust scattered on the floor. It was mid-morning so there were only a few customers in the place as it had just opened.

I could see that Walter was excited and he proudly pointed to a chalkboard on the bar which read: 'Fresh Oysters – 8 for £1'.

It was pretty obvious from Walter's face that we were supposed to be very impressed and he looked at us hoping to see the delight on our faces. Unfortunately, the opposite was true and we didn't know what to say. Christine and I loved sea food, but oysters were one supposed delicacy that wasn't on our wish list and I shivered as I looked at them. It had never crossed my mind to try them – just the look of them put me off.

What an awkward position to be in, poor old Walter had brought us to this lovely Guinness and Oyster Bar, a new concept in those days, where all the top people in Blackpool went, and here we were desperately trying to leg it through the door. Too late, and Walter proudly walked across to our table and put a plate of oysters in front of us. He was giving us something special.

Christine, tentatively and bravely managed to get one down but said she didn't want another.

My turn. The Irishman could see my reticence and came across and insisted that I would enjoy them and showed me what to do. I copied what he'd shown me and put the oyster on the palm of my hand, tilted my head upwards, opened my mouth and the oyster slid off its shell and into it. I was gipping like mad but thankfully it went down. What a bloody relief!

Suddenly, about two seconds later and without warning, I inadvertently coughed and in what seemed like slow motion the oyster shot out of my mouth; and I can see it now as it flew across the room, landing in the sawdust near the fireplace. You could've heard a pin drop and to make it worse still no one laughed. The barman, Walter and the other customers all just stared at the oyster lying in the sawdust and poor old Walter looked really, really embarrassed. The silence seemed to last for ever and I thought I was in the clear but the barman picked up the oyster, washed it under a tap behind the bar and passed the bloody thing back to me.

Meanwhile, Richard had started to cry and obviously wanted feeding; and so at that point we apologized to Walter and the barman and fled the pub in embarrassment. How anyone can eat those things is totally beyond me and as I'm writing this the thoughts of it still make me shudder.

After all that we set off home early – I'd had enough – so we decided to call in at my sister Bronnie's farm at Huddersfield for a cup of tea and some proper food, a jam sandwich would have been better than that rubbish. On the way there I told Christine to look out for Mr Mangle Worzel with the coffin on top of his car but he was nowhere to be seen. She thought I was kidding her anyway.

As we pulled into the farmyard I could see my brother-in-law John through the open door of the cow shed. He was wearing his usual green overalls and wellies, but he was also wearing long rubber gloves. Having heard the car pull up, he turned towards us and with an urgent voice said, 'Martyn, come and give me a hand if you can, Alan's gone to fetch the cows in ready for milking, but I've got a breach birth on my hands and I'm struggling.'

Running into the milking parlour, I grabbed a pair of overalls. They were a bit small but they'd just have to do as I knew that things were going to get messy.

A cow normally gives birth with the calf's head and front legs coming out first, but on this occasion I could see that the calf's back legs were partially out – in other words a breech birth.

Time was of the essence because if the umbilical cord broke whilst inside the cow the calf could die through lack of oxygen.

At that point John grabbed a fairly thick rope off a hook and proceeded to tie it round the hind legs of the calf. The cow itself was only small but the rear legs of the calf looked quite big. It was going to be hard work.

Both John and I braced ourselves and started to pull and after what seemed like a long time the calf started to slide out. As it did so the poor cow was bellowing, which was understandable when I saw the size of the calf she was giving birth to. Finally, the newcomer arrived, still attached to the umbilical cord and it dropped on to the straw that had been prepared for it. John removed the membrane from its mouth and rubbed its body with some straw to try to get it to breathe. The poor thing didn't move and so John opened its mouth and blew into it but still nothing. Having seen and done this many times before John picked the calf up and shook it just as though he was shaking a blanket and to our relief the calf started to breathe. In what seemed like no time at all its mum was licking it and it started to suckle. What a lovely sight to see. We were both sweating like stuck pigs but satisfied that we'd done a good job.

After a good swill down, we were both ready for a pot of tea and thankfully Bronnie, as per usual, put plenty of good snap on the table; which I for one was certainly ready for and then after tea we set off home with fresh eggs, milk and my favourite – home cured bacon – what a treat that was.

Before we left the farm I took Christine and little Richard to look at the newly-born calf. They both loved it, especially so when mum looked at us and gave a couple of 'moos' as if in thanks for helping with the delivery of her new 'baby' – nature at its best.

In the year that we got married, 1969, it had been a very bad winter and so much ice had accumulated on our local television mast at Emley Moor that the whole mast came crashing to the floor, destroying a small church as it did so. Luckily no one was hurt and within four days a small portable mast had replaced it. This in turn was replaced by a 200-metre mast which had been towed across the North Sea, from Sweden as far as I can remember. Many millions of people across the north of England had been affected by this loss, including ourselves. Watching anything on our small three-channelled TV was like being on an ocean wave; and you had to follow the picture as it went up and down the screen, which made you feel sea sick.

Near to this temporary tower, a brand new one had recently been built and had only been in operation for about a year. It was between Huddersfield and Thorpe Hesley where we lived so on our way home from the farm I decided to go and take a close look at it. It was absolutely enormous at 330 metres high, and it meant that, as from January 1971, tens of millions of people could now tune in to watch colour TV, that's if you could afford to buy one. I certainly wasn't one of those lucky people who could afford a colour set, especially now, as I'd just been informed by Christine that I was going to be a dad again. Wow, I couldn't wait and we were hoping for a little girl and we also wanted to call her Sally (our little princess).

It had been an interesting and enjoyable weekend away and I was certainly not looking forward to going back to work, but work is what paid the bills and that was the end of it. It was nice to get back to our own bed and I slept like a log, dreaming about cows; and then later a nightmare where I was standing at the bottom of Emley Moor TV mast and someone was pelting me with bloody oysters.

It was a usual busy Monday morning when I got back to work, with jobs that had come in over the weekend. Thefts of vehicles – thefts from vehicles – stolen bikes – shop and house break-ins – it was never ending.

Rick and John were both missing and the boss told me that he'd already sent them out on a rape enquiry. Apparently a fairly scruffy chap had solicited the services of a prostitute in the Wicker and he and a mate then drove her to some old garages within our division where full intercourse took place as agreed. The man's mate who had been standing outside the garage as sex was taking place must have got himself turned on by listening to what was happening. When his mate had finished the bloke simply entered the garage, forced himself on the woman and against her will had full sex with her. Trying to fend him off, she had badly scratched his face and for that he had beaten her up.

As the boss said, 'Just because she's a prostitute she still had the right to say 'no'.'

I looked at my crime diary and made notes of the several crimes that had been allocated to me to detect. I grabbed some statement forms and a car. I then went out on my own enquiries in Tinsley where there had been a spate of pedal cycle thefts. This took me a couple of hours or so and then I headed back to the office.

After climbing the stairs to the office I could see Rick and John interviewing a scruffy bloke whose face was a mass of scratches – they'd obviously caught the rapist. I recognized him as being a vegetable barrow boy who pitched up in the city; and I already knew that he had convictions for violence; and that he would be hard to deal with and wouldn't even admit to what day it was. He was being interviewed in the next office to me and a little while later as I was making some telephone enquiries, I saw John and Rick take Mr Nasty downstairs to the cells. He wouldn't admit to anything.

He had been identified by the complainant, a prostitute that I didn't know, from police mug shots. A statement from another prostitute who knew both men said that she'd seen her mate get into the car with them an hour before the rape took place. That and the fact that his face was a mass of scratches confirmed the allegation. It was him all right, but he wouldn't cough to it.

If someone admits to having committed the offence it makes our life easier than when we have to try and prove it. It also means that the complainant won't be put through the trauma of a trial if the offender goes on to plead guilty in court. But how were they to get an admission if Mr Nasty wouldn't even talk to them? As you've already worked out no doubt, taking skin samples from underneath the woman's fingernails and then comparing them with a sample taken from the man's face was one way. Semen samples from the vaginal swab was another but as detectives you also try other methods.

Enter Detective Constable Vicar. A nice genial man; and although rather plump and with a ruddy complexion he looked very smart in his dark suit and white clerical collar. The problem was that he was always drunk and sometimes asked to be locked up because of it. Today was one of those days and as he was unsteady on his feet he had to be guided into the cells by an officer in uniform – the same cell that Mr Nasty was occupying.

Rick and John had got nowhere by talking to Mr Nasty and asking questions, but Detective Constable Vicar had had some good results in the past, so it was worth half an hour or so of his time to try. His method of operation was quite simple. He'd be placed into a prison cell along with the other prisoner by a uniformed officer so as not to create suspicion. He would then pretend to be a drunken vicar and have a friendly chat and read a few lines from the Scriptures. If it looked as if the other prisoner had fallen for the subterfuge then our Detective

Constable Vicar would suggest that he should repent of his sins and admit to the nice policeman what he had done.

In the past I'd seen Detective Constable Vicar reduce some prisoners to tears and ready to admit whatever offence they were being interviewed for, but sadly on this occasion there was no divine intervention – Mr Nasty was having none of it so he was taken back upstairs to be re-interviewed.

I was in the other room when he was brought back up and I also knew what was happening and the fact that Rick and John were now struggling. I nipped downstairs and asked the Desk Sergeant to ring my extension upstairs in ten minutes time and asked that when I answered he should put the phone down.

Sure enough, ten minutes later the phone rang and I answered in a loud voice, 'Detective Constable Johnson,' and the phone went dead. Still with the phone in my hand and where I could be seen from the other room by the prisoner, I continued to talk as if I was in conversation with another person and I would pause every now and again for effect.

'Yes I think so' (Thirty second silence); 'Bloody hell that does sound serious' (Ten seconds silence).

'Yes doctor, I'll ask them' (another ten seconds silence); 'I'll get back in touch, okay doctor, thank you,' (Ten seconds silence); 'Yes of course I know it's urgent. Bye.'

At that point I put the phone down and ran into the other room where John and Rick were talking to Mr Nasty, and I pointed to him.

'Is that the bloke who's in for rape?' I asked in an urgent voice.

'Yes, why?' asked John.

'I've just had the hospital on the line – if he's done it they want him at the hospital immediately,' I said.

'He says he's not done it,' said Rick.

'Well, you need to catch the bloke that has then, and quickly – they've examined the woman who's been raped at the hospital and she's got a new and rare strain of syphilis which could prove fatal if not treated within 24 hours of catching it,' I said.

With that I walked back into the other room and positioned myself so that I could see any reactions to what I had said.

Rick and John knew me well enough to know where I was coming from. I could just see Mr Nasty squirming in his chair and looking at his watch, so I nipped further back into the room and chuckled to myself – would it work?

A few minutes later I could hear a commotion coming from the other room and I heard Rick say sharply, 'Why didn't you admit it before – and no, I'm not taking you to hospital until you've signed a statement admitting your guilt – okay?'

The now, not so clever Mr Nasty said, 'Can we please get on with it quick, I don't feel well, I need to go to the hospital.'

I could hear what was going off and when he'd written and signed his statement I nipped back into the other room and addressed Rick and John.

'Sorry lads – there's been some confusion at the hospital and they gave me details of a different woman – the one who was raped hasn't got syphilis after all.'

At that point Mr Nasty turned very nasty but I can't think for the life of me why!

We were joined by Detective Constable Vicar who removed his clerical collar and put it back in the drawer where it lived, ready for next time; and at that point Mr Nasty started to rant all over again. He knew he'd been duped.

Both the skin and semen tests were later done and both proved conclusively that Mr Nasty was the rapist. He pleaded guilty at court and was sentenced to two years in prison, which he justly deserved, and the expression – 'if you catch a weasel asleep, piss in its ear mate' came to mind.

CHAPTER 18

You Can't Win 'Em All

What a bloody mess – if I hadn't seen it with my own eyes I wouldn't have believed it.

Rick and I were both on afters, working the 3pm to 11pm shift. Sundays were usually quiet, which suited us down to the ground. It would soon be Christmas and everyone would be getting ready for the big day itself. It was an expensive time of year and although, like everyone else, I enjoyed Christmas and its festivities, I was always glad when it was over. At that point I would look forward to the end of March by which time I hoped that my bank statement would be coloured black and not red.

Everyone and their grandmothers would be shopping and looking for a bargain over the next few days when shopping would really start, unlike today, several weeks earlier. Burglars, pick-pocketers, and shoplifters were just like everyone else at Christmas. The first two would try to steal your well-earned cash, whilst a shop lifter would steal and then try to sell you a bargain. Christine had dragged me kicking and screaming to the city centre the day before; and even though the atmosphere was electric it was absolute bedlam; and I'd been glad to get home – luckily for me there was no Meadowhall shopping mall in those days.

At about 7pm and after taking statements and making enquiries about four or five house break-ins on the Flower Estate at Firth Park, we decided to nip into the Firth Park Hotel to see if we could 'sniff' anything out. Pub landlords always kept an ear to the ground and usually knew what was going off. Joe, the landlord, was a nice and amiable guy, but who could handle himself if anyone messed him about. After pulling us a glass of beer each we were chatting about Christmas and the icy cold wind and weather that had kicked in about a week earlier.

At that point in walked a small old lady with a torch in her hand and a worried look on her face.

'What's up love?' said Joe.

'Have you seen anything of Joyce, today?' she asked.

'No, but she was in last night and I sent her home because she'd had one or two too many – why?' asked Joe.

'I can hear a baby crying in the house, but no one's answering the door – I'm worried sick about it,' she said.

Joe looked across the bar at Rick and me with a look on his face that said, 'Over to you gents.'

'Has anyone got a key to the house, love, or does a relative live nearby?' I asked,hopefully.

'Nobody that I know of love, but what's it got to do with you anyway?' she replied, indignantly. 'Who are you?'

Rick showed her his warrant card and told her who we were and then she said, 'Sorry mister, but we don't normally see men in suits round here,' which made us both chuckle.

Something wasn't right, so we borrowed a torch from Joe and followed the old lady back through the freezing wind to the house concerned. The house itself was an end terrace with an 'off-shot' kitchen and it was in total darkness. The old lady was right and we could both hear a baby crying and from the noise that the poor thing was making it sounded desperate. Urgent action was needed, mum must be either dead or in a collapsed condition.

All the curtains were open but Rick couldn't see much with only a small torch so he ran back to the car in the hope that there was one there – but nothing. Both doors to the house were locked and a quick inspection of the sash windows with a torch that Rick had managed to scrounge from the nearby petrol station proved to be locked as well.

All this had taken about three or four minutes and as parents ourselves we were more than desperate to get inside to help the poor child. I can assure you that if that back door had been made of solid steel I would have smashed through it. The adrenalin kicked in and I ran across the yard and hit the door with my shoulder and smashed it clean off its hinges on contact – we were in.

As I picked myself up off the kitchen floor a yelping dog shot past me and into the yard. The smell of dog shit hit me in a big way, which wasn't surprising as I later found out that my suit was covered in it from falling on to the floor.

Where was the poor child? After fumbling about I found the light switch but when I pressed it – nothing. At this point Rick pushed past me. 'I bet the shillings run out of the slot,' he said as he made his way to the cellar head and then down into the cellar itself. I could hear him put a coin or two in the meter and as he climbed back up the cellar steps I tried the light switch again – bingo, at last we could see.

What a bloody mess – but first things first. Our priority was obviously the child who was still crying but we couldn't see it. We both ran into the living room (sorry, I've just had to put my pen down for a few minutes as the memory has brought it all back). Near the door was a cot, inside which was standing a little girl of about twelve months of age. Both she and the little blankets in the cot were covered in dried up poo and her hair was matted in it; and to me her little legs looked bowed – both Rick and I could have wept when we saw her. Also in the cot was a baby's feeding bottle that was full of bright green mould and a tiny drop of sour milk. These observations took seconds; and while Rick tried to pacify the frail little girl I started to search the house for her mum.

Gingerly, I entered the filthy bathroom – nothing; and it was the same in the two bedrooms. Where the bloody hell was she? Surely she must be here somewhere, so I went back downstairs. Near to what was left of the door was a zinc mop bucket full of what looked like human excrement; and dog muck was all over the kitchen floor. At least now with there being no door the revolting smell had abated a bit. I suddenly realized that I hadn't checked the outside toilet but there was nothing there either.

As I once more picked my way through the dog muck it made me gip as I went to wash my hands, only to discover that the water pipes were frozen up. What the hell is going off here, I thought. The landlord of the pub had told us that he'd seen her last night but where was she now? The staples which would hold the door bolts were still in situ on the door frame so the bolts had not been fastened when I forced the door open, neither could I see a door key anywhere. The woman must have locked the door from the outside and then gone where? It could be anywhere.

Rick had, meanwhile, nipped to the old lady's house a couple of doors away and borrowed a blanket; and had then taken the little girl back to the house where at least she was warm. The old lady had also managed to borrow a baby's bottle and a couple of rusks from a neighbour who had children and at last the baby was being fed and had stopped crying; good for you and well done lady, I thought.

As Rick and I walked back into the house and the stinking squalor, we were followed back in by a scruffy mongrel bitch, obviously the one that had bolted past me as I entered the house. At the same time we heard a quiet whimpering noise coming from a large chest of drawers in the living room. As Rick slowly opened the second drawer from the bottom we could see two emaciated puppy dogs looking up at us.

Both Rick and I were cursing big style and we were absolutely livid. What sort of a hell hole were we in? Who could leave a child alone in the dark, with nothing to eat or drink and no heating, light or water and with both human and animal excrement all over the place? We could have both wept for the poor little child.

A further quick check of the house showed that everywhere was a stinking mess and we couldn't even see a pram or a push chair in the house; and we both doubted that the baby had ever left her cot. There didn't appear to be any gents clothing in the house but in one of the bedrooms we spotted quite a few ladies dresses which looked brand new and expensive to us.

Rick contacted the office via the car radio and asked them to contact the Royal Society for the Prevention of Cruelty to Children with a request for the on duty welfare officer to attend the house as soon as possible. At the same time he also asked that the RSPCA attend as well in order to remove the dogs. Within three quarters of an hour the RSPCA had been and taken the dogs away but unbelievably there was no one on call out from the RSPCC. At that last news Rick and I went ballistic, what were we supposed to do now? For all we knew, mum, if she could be called that, could be dead somewhere and we were stuck with an infant that needed proper care and attention. Enough was enough, bollocks to fancy rules and regulations. We needed to act now.

After picking up the baby girl from the old ladies house and thanking her for the brilliant help she had given us, we were off. By now it was snowing which didn't make the five-mile journey to the Sheffield Children's Hospital any easier, but nevertheless we managed to get her there. At long last the poor little thing was going to get some well-deserved tender, loving care – or was she?

'Are you the father?' asked a lady administrator, as she covered her nose from the smell of my suit.

'No, I'm not,' and I showed her my police warrant card.

'I'm sorry but we can't treat her without her parent's details and consent,' she said.

'I'm also sorry because we don't know the parents and neither do we know where they are,' I explained.

'How do I know that you haven't kidnapped her?' she said.

By this stage there was steam coming out of my ears as we'd already told her the circumstances behind us being there at the hospital in the beginning. I was just about to blow my top, big style, when a doctor spotted the baby girl and intervened.

'It's all right Mrs _____, I've heard what these two gentlemen have said and I also understand their predicament. You did the right thing Mrs _____, but now I'll take over.'

'Thank goodness for that.' And after leaving our contact details with the hospital we were off again.

On the way back to the nick we called back in at 'Poo palace' but still no one was there. Where on earth was the woman and what sort of a person was she to leave a baby like that? It was totally beyond our comprehension; but she just had to be found.

Joe was just closing the pub doors at about 10.50pm when we pulled up. We both had our fingers crossed, but soon uncrossed them again when Joe asked us if we fancied a swift pint. That was like music to our ears and we were in like a shot. Joe kept wrinkling up his nose as we stood at the bar. We didn't realize just how much we stank and as we'd been in that state for the last four hours we must have got immune to it ourselves.

'Joe, did you say earlier on tonight that you chucked this Joyce woman out of the pub the night before?' asked Rick.

'Yes, she can sup as good as any bloke, but last night she was staggering all over the place so I turned her out – why?'

Ignoring the question, Rick continued: 'What family has she got?'

'None that I'm aware of, she lived with a chap up until a couple of years ago but that's all that I know.'

'What about kids?' Rick asked, which made Joe chuckle.

'You must be joking, she's not fit enough to keep a pet hamster, never mind a nipper; she's always half pissed,' and he chuckled again.

'What does she do for a living?' I asked Joe; and I could see him shuffle and he also grabbed his beer and lowered his eyes whilst at the same time he shrugged his shoulders.

'Have you asked Mary, the old lady who lives next door to her?' said Joe.

'Yes, and she says she keeps herself to herself and only knocked on her door today because she could hear a baby crying all the time.' I said, and I continued, 'come on Joe, tell us what she does.'

He hesitated but went on to say, 'I haven't told you this, okay? But the word on the street is that she's the best shoplifter in town; if you want something then she'll get it and she seems to do all right with it.'

So that's where all the new dresses had come from, which was the least of our concerns. All we had to do now was to find the woman who had stolen them – where could she be? We'd managed to make sure that the baby was being properly looked after and the same with the dogs, but where was she?

The only bloke that we knew who had met her was Joe so I thought it best to tell him about the evening's events and the fact that 'Joyce' was missing. He was absolutely aghast at what we'd told him and simply said, 'If she's had a good day and has nicked plenty of gear she'll be trying to flog it in the pubs. If she's already sold it all, she'll have plenty of cash and that's when she gets pissed.'

No real clues there then! So once more we checked 'Poo palace' – nothing; so we left a note on the door to tell 'Joyce' to contact the police and then we went back to the station. She'd been missing now for over 24 hours and Joe had been the last one to see her when he'd thrown her out of the pub the night before. I was just about to ring the children's hospital when the Duty Sergeant brought a chap upstairs to the office. It was the child welfare officer who we'd tried to get hold of several hours earlier. He'd come to the station after he had visited Joyce's house and seen the note on the door that we'd left some half an hour ago – so why didn't he come to the house when he'd been asked to do, I wondered?

He didn't look too pleased and he told us that he'd travelled from the other side of the city to the house only to find that no one was there. Rick and I looked at each other as we recognized another 'jobsworth'. They know all the answers but are never there at the sharp end of the stick when urgent decisions have to be made. As we told him about the house and the missing mum the cheeky bugger interrupted and said in a frustrated manner, 'Where's the child now, I need to examine her?' So we told him what we had done and where the baby was. His eyes opened wide in amazement and he said, 'You mean to tell me that you have kidnapped that little girl?'

'If that's what you want to call it mate, yes we have – let's ring the doctor at the hospital and before you get your knickers in a twist you can talk to him,' I said.

Rick could see my anger and had already got the doctor on the phone. He passed the phone over to the 'jobsworth' so that he could speak to the doctor himself. As he was in conversation with the doctor at the children's hospital he kept nodding his head and writing something down on bits of paper. As he came off the phone he looked at our not so happy faces and said, 'I do apologize, the doctor has praised your actions and explained that you had no other options. Unfortunately the poor little girl is suffering from hypothermia, scabies and impetigo. She's also suffering from rickets and malnutrition. The doctor thinks that she may have spent all or most of her life in the cot. If you find the mother please let me know.'

We told him that there was no pram or push chair in the house so now we knew why, she'd probably never left the house as the doctor said. With that he left us and went to the children's hospital.

Rick decided to ring the Charge Office in town to see if a female had been locked up for drunkenness or shoplifting, whilst I checked hospital admissions over the last 24 hours. Sod's law being what it is, a night duty policeman had stumbled across a youngish woman who reeked of alcohol lying on the pavement at about 11.15pm the night before. Incredibly, this incident was roughly half a mile from where 'Joyce' lived. She was unconscious and had a gash on her head consistent with hitting the wall that she was lying next to when she was found. The policeman had phoned for an ambulance and she had been admitted to the Northern General Hospital suffering from concussion and possible amnesia.

It was decided that I nip to the hospital whilst Rick started a full report on everything that had happened. By now it was about 2am and when I arrived there it was fairly quiet. I had no idea what this woman looked like so after explaining who I was and why I was there I was taken to the ward.

The woman we suspected of being 'Joyce' had a handbag and the staff nurse and I went through it. There was no identification in it but plenty of cash and what we did find was a door key.

This might be the clue we needed to find out if this was 'Joyce', and half an hour later back at the house, I tried the key in the lock and it opened. Bingo – what a relief, we'd found her.

Back at the office I informed the doctor at the children's hospital and also the child welfare officer, and told them where 'Joyce' was. It had been another long shift but the satisfaction for Rick and I was off the top of the scale, knowing that the baby was now being properly cared for.

The night shift Sergeant said that he'd arrange to make the house secure and with nothing more that we could do, Rick and I went home, both well and truly knackered.

The baby was later taken into care by the welfare people and 'Joyce' signed herself out of hospital the following evening. A few days later she was charged with neglect of a child, neglect of animals and also shoplifting. We also contacted Social Services in the hope that they could also help 'Joyce' with her own problems.

About three months later Rick and I were called to court to give evidence against 'Joyce'. When she arrived at court she looked very smart and was carrying a fairly large teddy bear. The magistrate heard all the evidence from all parties concerned, including the mother who was pleading to have her baby back. Social Services had re-housed her and they told the magistrate that she had mended her ways. They even pointed to the teddy bear which they said was proof of the mother's affection for her daughter. BULLSHIT, bloody bullshit.

Half an hour later 'Joyce' was all smiles, the magistrate felt sorry for her and her hard upbringing. A three-month suspended prison sentence followed and she was told that her baby could be returned to her later that same day. Outside court I sarcastically asked 'Joyce' where she had bought the teddy bear from. Listen to this. 'I haven't, I called in at Redgates Toy Shop before I came to court. I only "borrowed" it and it's done the trick.' With that she put the Teddy on a public bench and, laughing, walked away.

We just couldn't be bothered to do anything about it anymore. The doctor had said in court that it was one of the most prolonged and serious cases of child neglect that he had ever come across.

I like to think that Rick and I had done our bit on that occasion, and we both thought it a shame that someone else hadn't done their job properly.

About six months after getting her baby back, 'Joyce' was apparently up to her old ways once more when she was caught shoplifting in town. It wasn't our case but from what I can gather the baby was once more taken into care; and that is the last that I ever heard of them.

CHAPTER 19

Happy Christmas

A couple of days after 'Joyce's' baby episode and three months before her court appearance, Rick and I were still on afters, working the 3pm to 11pm shift.

As I drove to work through the light snow I was thinking about 'old Fred', the tramp or gentleman of the road as he preferred to be introduced as (see chapter 15, *What's Tha Up To?*). I had first met Fred about five years ago when a group of young men were picking on him and pushing him about, thinking that they were big shots. At that time Fred would be about sixty years old and the lads didn't like it when I intervened, even though I was off duty. As an ex-blacksmith I was a big, strong lad then and I managed to put three of them down in quick succession. The other two legged it; and I ended up losing another tooth and gained a shiner. It was worth it, I hated bullies.

During the year Fred would wander the country, doing seasonal odd jobs for farmers or fruit and hop growers. He did his own thing and had never drawn a penny in benefits. He ate what he could catch, such as fish, rabbits, ducks, pheasants and squirrels; and, as well as being fit, Fred was very happy with his lot. For shelter he used barns, sheds and sometimes hedge bottoms but he kept himself clean by washing in streams or rivers.

I'd been thinking about him for the last two weeks which was when winter had kicked in and the odd snow fall had covered most of the North. Over the past five years Fred would make his way up country and head for Sheffield. I always knew when he'd arrived because he called into the nick and left a message for me. He was later than usual and I was a bit concerned for his safety, but luckily I had no need to be worried as there on my desk, when I arrived for work, was a note: 'Fred's in Town – you know where he is.'

After signing on duty I walked up to 'Banners' (John Banners Ltd department store) on Attercliffe Road and bought the widest and longest black belt that I could find. As I walked back down the 'Cliffe I could hear, even before I saw him, Ernest, who sold fruit and veg from a barrow.

'Come on missis, carrots 3d a pound – as big as your mister's, plus two free 'taters to match'. Ernest was a great bloke and I always stopped and had a laugh with him, but on this occasion I didn't have the time to stop. I was late for school and didn't want to get the cane like I used to get when I was late myself as a kid.

I'd arranged to meet the headmaster at the Dr John Worrall School on Maltby Street, and by this time the kids would have left school for the day and gone home. As I walked into his office I could see a red Father Christmas suit and a long white beard hung up on a peg. Just the job I thought to myself as I nipped to the toilets and tried it on. After shoving a couple of cushions into my shirt and just managing to fasten the large black belt that I'd just bought – I grabbed the school hand bell and swung it and, 'Ho, Ho, Hoed,' as I looked into the mirror.

If the real Father Christmas was ugly then I certainly looked the part.

Dr John Worrall's School was a 'Special School' and was attended by children, some of which had problems. Four years previously and when I was still on the beat I discovered that no one dared play Father Christmas anymore because some of the kids were unruly and could also be violent. I knew that this was true as the year before a ten-year-old boy had stabbed a teacher in the arm with a knife.

All kids love to see Father Christmas and, as far as I was concerned, these kids were no different. Some of them had both parents, some had one and some others none at all, and I felt that if I could brighten up their lives even a little bit, then they'd enjoy Father Christmas just as you and I did as nippers.

That's when I volunteered for the job and in two day's time it would be my fifth year – at least I hadn't got the 'sack'!

Back at the office I caught up with some paperwork and then ate my snap, tinned salmon sarnies – what a treat. After that I went to see if Fred was in his normal winter-holiday resort, the brickworks on Makin Road just off Darnall Road itself.

I climbed up the wooden steps to the top level and said hello to the night watchman, old Tom. I always found it fascinating when I visited. Tom had a little cabin and in it were a chair, table, wireless and kettle. Stretching away in front of this cabin for quite a distance was a red-brick floor covered in dust; and set into the floor at regular intervals were round iron lids about six inches across and with a hook on them. There were dozens of them and underneath were the brick kilns. Every time the temperature of the kilns dropped to a certain level it was Tom's job to lift the lids and drop a small quantity of coal down each hole which glowed red hot when opened. I could never stand it for too long, it was too hot for me. After a chat I asked if Fred was downstairs and he answered in the affirmative.

Back down stairs I walked through one of the open archways and towards the kilns. It was lovely and warm and also quiet and my feet didn't make a sound as I walked through the warm sand on the floor. Fred was fast asleep when I found him, standing up with his arms looped over a clothes line that he'd rigged up between two hooks. I'd seen this before in a registered 'doss' (lodging) house in Barnsley when I was younger where a sign said '1/- per night for a bed' – but if you 'dossed' on a clothes line it was free.

This is where the expression 'I could sleep on a clothes line' comes from.

I quietly coughed and Fred woke up with a start. We shook hands and exchanged greetings – we were glad to see each other again. Under the old Vagrancy Act, Fred's stay in the Brick Kiln was illegal but old Tom, the night watchman, wasn't bothered about it and neither was I, he wasn't hurting a soul. Fred was a grafter and last winter Tom had fixed him up with quite a bit of work; and the kilns were his home until about the middle of March when he would set off on his long walk south. Wiping his enamel 'billy can' with a bit of rag, he offered me a drink of tea out of its lid. I've always been a 'tea belly' and after gritting my teeth I managed to get it down without gipping, which made him laugh. While I had a fag, he filled his home-made cherry wood pipe with some sort of fern leaves and then sat in the warm sand while we swapped the latest news. Just before I left and seeing that he was wearing a decent looking pair of trousers and a jacket, which an old farmer had given him, I told him that I needed to see him at 2pm the following day at the police station. He didn't ask why – but gave me a quizzical look when I told him to be as clean and spruced up as possible. He trusted me, so I knew that he'd be there.

After finishing work and as I was driving home I kept chuckling to myself – a good idea or a bad idea, we'd have to wait and see.

Bang on 2pm Fred arrived at the nick – he certainly looked decent with his long white hair and white beard, a blue shirt with a red neckerchief tucked into the top of it. He was better dressed, nearly, than I was, but he wasn't too happy when I gave him a squirt of aftershave which I'd brought with me just in case he smelled.

When I told him that I was playing Father Christmas at the local school in an hour's time and that he was going to be Santa's reindeer keeper, he nearly dropped bow legged and started to stutter. I'd earlier explained to the headmaster what I was hoping to do and he was all for it. Here we go, I thought as we sneaked into the school by the back door so as not to be seen by the children. Fred couldn't believe what was happening as one of the staff put a red loose fitting tunic over his jacket and then put a green felt hat on his head.

With that and his long white beard and red glowing cheeks he really looked the part.

When all the mums and dads had taken their seats and then all the children were lined up and told to sit on the floor, the headmaster asked the children if they wanted to meet Father Christmas and his reindeer shepherd. That was our cue and everyone cheered and shouted as Fred and I walked into the hall. I was carrying a small sack of presents in one hand and ringing the school bell with the other. Fred was behind and carrying a larger sack full of presents in one hand and waving a large carrot about in the other – he was loving it and lapping up the atmosphere.

As the children started to sing *Away in a Manger* I could feel myself getting all emotional. By the time they'd got to the end of the carol, I turned to look at Fred and I could see tears running down his cheeks. It made me remember the poor baby in the cot three days ago and I ended up doing the same as Fred.

After the carols it was present time and we were mobbed by the kids trying to be first in the queue to get theirs. They were so excited and it was magical to see them so happy. I had my beard pulled a few times as I quickly handed out the presents until the small sack was empty. A minute later I was in hysterics as I watched a queue of kids in front of poor Fred. Every third or fourth kid gave a good tug on his real white beard thinking that it was false, and he was jumping about in all directions. He wasn't loving it now.

A minute or two later it was all over and we joined the crowd of kids at the trestle tables which were weighed down with sandwiches, cakes and trifles. When Fred saw all the snap on the table, especially the delicacies, his eyes nearly popped out of his head. He couldn't believe his luck.

The headmaster and staff couldn't thank Fred and me enough for helping out. It had all worked out well for them and they even invited us both back again for the following Christmas. It was the last day of school before the Christmas break and as 'the Star of the Show' and I left the school, and with Fred clutching two big bags full of leftover food, he started to sing carols to himself. It was obvious that he'd enjoyed his new found stardom, his chest was puffed out with pride and he had a huge grin stretching from ear to ear.

'Brilliant – brilliant,' he kept saying on our way back to the brick kiln. He then continued, 'but if I'd have known what you'd wanted me to do I wouldn't have turned up, but I've loved it, thanks Martyn – book us in for next year, them little kids were great,' and he was laughing his shepherd's head off.

Christmas was always an awkward time at the station because everyone wanted the day off to be with their families. Since joining the job I'd always volunteered to work Christmas Day. For the first seven years and when I was in uniform I was single. On this occasion I was married and little Richard was only a few months old, so I once again, volunteered to work on Christmas Day so that another detective who had older children could have the day off instead.

My turn next year, I thought.

Travelling to work down the M1 from Thorpe Hesley at 6.30am on the 25th December was a weird experience. Although only one junction down the motorway, I never saw another vehicle travelling in either direction. It was the same on the under section of the Tinsley Viaduct and after turning right onto Attercliffe Common it was the same there. All the works were closed down and even Albert and May's paper shop, next to the Lambpool pub was closed. Attercliffe was like a ghost town and even though the roads and pavements were covered in a thin layer of snow there wasn't a tyre track or footprint to be seen.

As I pulled the car up near the back of the nick I noticed another car pull up a good few yards behind me. I turned to see who it was and as I did so I saw the other driver get out of his car and beckon me towards him. I recognized him immediately and shouted, 'Happy Christmas Ronnie' – and I knew from experience what would be coming next.

Ronnie was a great bloke and I had a lot of admiration for him. He and his wife were the famous singing and dancing cabaret act working the theatres and night clubs the length and breadth of the country, under the name of, 'Ronnie Dukes and Ricky Lee'. They even played at the London Palladium Royal Variety Performance in 1974; and Ronnie was on *This is Your Life* hosted by Eamonn Andrews back in the 1970s. Ronnie was an incredible dancer and Ricky was a fabulous impersonator and singer. Ricky's mum played the piano on stage for them; and she was the butt of Ronnie's 'mother-in-law' jokes; and she was famous for her deadpan face. It's been said that he had the best mother-in-law gags in the business.

Ronnie was a good Rotherham lad and Ricky was born and bred in Attercliffe, in the house that I was now standing outside.

Several years earlier I'd become pals with Ricky's brother Tommy and on more than one occasion, when I was on night shift, I would catch them in the early hours of the morning coming back from one of their long distance gigs. They'd invite me to have a beer with them at Ricky's mum's house; and I always thought it 'polite' to accept, which helped them wind down after a long nights work; and on more than one occasion I have staggered back to the nick in the early hours of the morning – what a treat.

'Come on in Martyn, for a Christmas drink,' Ronnie said.

'Not this morning Ronnie, I can't, thanks. I'm the only detective working the Division and I might end up with a serious job today. Anyway, you're late back, where the hell have you been?' I asked.

'I've just driven up from bloody London and I'm absolutely knackered; it was a late cabaret show and we stopped to see Christmas in, that's why we're so late back,' Ronnie replied. 'Come on just have one Martyn.'

'Okay Ronnie, but just the one,' I said.

Ricky and her mum Peggy made a cup of tea while Ronnie and I each opened a bottle of Newcastle Brown Ale. He was a really funny bloke and I could have listened to him all day but it was no good I had to get to work. I was still laughing at some of his mother-in-law jokes when I made my way back to the nick.

I'd love to see their act one more time. The versatility and energy that Ronnie put into his act had to be seen to be believed and sweat would pour out of him in a big way. The glamorous Ricky and her 'deadpan' mum at the piano complemented Ronnie's energy and I'll defy anybody in those days to better their act, no wonder they became so famous and well liked.

Back at the nick all was quiet, which was decidedly odd; and I ended up looking at the telephone in the office and waiting for it to ring as opposed to a normal day when I would dread it ringing. By dinner time with nothing happening I decided to nip home and have my dinner there with Christine and Richard. One of the presents we'd bought him was a Sooty money box in the form of a Kelly but he was far more interested when playing with the wrapping paper. I only stayed three quarters of an hour and drove back to work to finish my shift at 3pm. I can honestly say that it was a first for me with nothing whatsoever happening on an eight-hour shift and I was glad for everybody else's sake out there that at least there had been nothing serious happen in our division; and as I drove home and put the wireless on at 3pm I even managed to listen to the Queen's speech. At the end of the speech she wished everyone a happy Christmas and I shouted back, 'the same to you Ma'am and to everyone else. Happy Christmas!'

CHAPTER 20

Where's a 'Copper' When You Need One?

I've always had a fascination with old things, especially those that were made many years before I was born. Who made them? Who used them? Why did they make them and so on?

At the age of seven we moved to live in one of the first houses to be built on a new council estate in Darfield but further up the village where I found a new playmate called Roy Williamson. There were still a lot of houses to be built and a large area was a building site; and my dad told me not to play in the long slit trenches which formed a large cut in the ground in the shape of an oblong. These cuts in the ground were deep and were to form the footings of the new houses. They didn't look dangerous to me or Roy but they did look interesting to explore and within ten minutes of being told not to Roy and I were in the trenches.

As we were running along the bottom of one of the trenches I spotted something like an old orange-coloured pot sticking out from the side of the trench and I stopped to look. The pot was cracked and as I gently pulled at one of the shards of pottery a stream of green and silver discs fell out and into the bottom of the trench. We were only kids and, not knowing what they were, we started throwing them all over the place. After a little while we got fed up and as I looked at one of the silver discs I could see somebody's head on one side and on the other a picture of two children sitting underneath what looked to be a wolf (which later turned out to be a depiction of Romulus and Remus suckling from the she wolf and who later supposedly founded Rome).

At the time we didn't realize what we'd found and we were still throwing them in different directions. We must have unwittingly attracted the attention of other people and all of a sudden I heard a loud voice shout, 'What are you two little monkeys doing down there?' Both Roy and I looked up and there looking down at us was the biggest policeman that I'd ever seen and to me as a seven-year-old he looked twenty feet tall. At this point the policeman leaned down into the trench, grabbed us by our shirt collars and hauled us out.

My dad arrived and I got a 'scutch' round the ear for being in the trench in the first place. A short while after I'd been hauled out, other people arrived together with a chap with a trilby hat, dark, rimmed glasses and a long coat – somebody said that he was an archaeologist, which didn't mean a thing to me at that time. I didn't know who he was but he went down a short ladder and into the trench gathering up some of the things that we'd been throwing about. People seemed excited but Roy and I were terrified and knew that we shouldn't have been there.

It later transpired that we had found and disturbed a hoard of somewhere between two and three thousand silver and copper coins dating to the Roman period, about 2,000 years ago. The coins were eventually taken away and some ended up in Sheffield Museum, but today some of them are on display at the new Experience Barnsley museum, which I'm dead chuffed about. From then on I was hooked on two things: the police force and local history; the latter of which I've been researching into for the last sixty-five years.

For as long as I can remember I have collected and bartered with things such as conkers, marbles and old coins and my fascination with old things has never waned. As a toddler my grandma used to take me to antique shops in Barnsley where she would buy me bits and bobs which I liked the look of. Another distant relative had a small second-hand shop in Wombwell and I loved nothing better than rooting round and looking for interesting things.

In 1965 when I started courting Christine, I purchased my first metal detector through a mail order catalogue called Exchange and Mart. Much to Christine's annoyance, instead of taking her out for tea to a nice restaurant or pub I used to drag her through the muddy fields along with my metal detector. The metal detector wasn't anywhere near as good as the machines of today but nevertheless I found loads of Victorian pennies and halfpennies, as well as bits of lead, old horseshoes, cartridge cases and bottle tops. For years I used that machine but never met up with anyone else who had one, the hobby of metal detecting was in its infancy in those days.

It's a wonderful hobby and in 1979 I bought myself a more up-to-date model which vastly improved my finds rate. In 1985 my local pub in Wentworth, the Rockingham Arms, decided to hold an event to celebrate the 40th anniversary of Victory in Europe Day. The then owners of the pub, Joe Foster, Jerry Wade and Nigel Hague (Nigel is the father of William Hague, the former Foreign Secretary), three great blokes, must have negotiated a deal with the brewery and it was decided that beer would be sold at the vastly reduced rate of four old pennies (4d) a pint which would have been the cost of a pint of beer on VE Day itself in 1945. The catch was that the beer had to be purchased with the old 'copper' pennies themselves but which had been out of circulation for many a year. For this reason I suddenly had people knocking on my door both from the village and beyond who were aware of my metal detecting exploits in the past. I became the most popular man in town as I'd accumulated hundreds of old copper pennies over the years.

Loads of people, including my police pals, attended the event with pockets full of old pennies donated by yours truly and we all got into the spirit of it by dressing up in 1940s clothes. As far as I can remember, between us we supped the pub dry. What a night that was and I don't think many of us arrived for work the day after. It gave the phrase 'where's a copper when you need one?' a totally different meaning.

When reading this aforementioned story some of you have probably thought to yourself why is Martyn talking about his hobby of metal detecting? There is a reason for this; and if you bear with me all will become clear and I think that you will find it both interesting and thought provoking.

In 1972 Christine and I were very fortunate when our beautiful daughter Sally was born. Both Richard and Sally grew up from toddlers to teenagers and made us proud. We taught them about local history and nature in the hope that they derived as much pleasure from it as we had done. They also took to metal detecting and on quite a few weekend mornings we could be seen wandering in the early morning mist at the side of the River Trent down in North Lincolnshire.

On the way back we would pick up a Chinese take-away and then settle in front of our log fire to warm ourselves through. Richard went on to be a brilliant artist whilst Sally became a nursery nurse. As soon as Sally was old enough she decided to become a blood donor and to date has donated just short of fifty pints. It is something that we are very proud of as I myself over the last twenty years have received three blood transfusions.

When Richard moved to attend Birmingham University, Sally and I continued to metal detect on odd occasions. She had grown into a beautiful adult and I think she still went out with me just to please me.

Wentworth has two pubs: 'The Rock', as we locals call it (Rockingham Arms), and the George and Dragon, where one of my great uncles was the landlord in the 1880s. Both pubs have been my regular haunts over the past forty-odd years and some of the laughs and incidents that I've been involved in, in both pubs, are truly amazing.

In about 1983 a youngish chap of about thirty started to occasionally use both pubs. He was always on his own and never stayed long. Quite a few of us passed the time of day with him and discovered that his name was James and that he was a part-time taxi driver who lived not many miles away.

James was a nice pleasant chap and sometime after we had first met he approached me and we spoke about metal detecting. He was really interested and asked if he could have a go himself. He was lucky, as some friends of mine had arranged with a farmer at nearby Swinton to search his land in a couple of weeks time. I kitted James out with a spare machine and on the appointed day James, Sally and I joined the rest of my pals at the farm. We all set off in the hope of finding Roman coins, as the field was adjacent to the old Roman road. I kept an eye on his progress throughout the day but he was okay and searching alongside Sally, who knew the ropes.

We all got together at the end of the day and between us we had found about twenty Roman coins and a few hammered silver ones, all in all, a good day.

James had enjoyed it and over the next three months or so asked if he could join Sally and me on another day out. Sods law being what it is it would be another few weeks before we went out again and once again he enjoyed the day. I used to see him about once a month and he would always ask how Sally was, and then after knowing him for about five years I didn't see him for quite a while.

The next time that I saw him was in the George and Dragon when he was wearing a nice suit. He looked very smart, and also knew it, and I laughed as I saw him eyeing up the pretty girls in the pub. He never stayed long and an hour later he was gone.

After that his visits seemed to slow down and got less and less, or at least I didn't see him when I was in the pub. The next time that I saw him was a few years later when he explained that his work had kept him very busy and he didn't have time to call in like he used to do. James told me that he'd got himself a very good job at a printing firm a few miles away and that he had also become a Freemason and he puffed his chest out with pride as he told me. He had certainly bettered himself and seemed to have come on a long way from being a part-time taxi driver twenty years ago when I first met him.

In March 2006 and maybe six months after I'd last seen James in the Rockingham Arms, I was at home when a mate of mine telephoned me to ask if I'd seen the local Sheffield newspaper.

'No, why,' I said, 'what's in it?'

'Never mind what's in it, just go and buy it and read it for yourself,' he said.

As I flicked through the pages of the paper outside the village shop, I was cursing. What was I supposed to see to cause my mate to be so secretive, it could be absolutely anything, so I turned back to the front page.

'Notorious' shoe rapist' arrested in South Yorkshire', so I lit a fag and read on. I just could not believe my eyes at what I read next – it was James. I was in deep shock and nearly got knocked down by a car as I crossed the road to go home. I just couldn't take it in, that such an apparently nice, ordinary, everyday sort of a bloke could be the monster that they were talking about. He seemed so placid. They must have got it wrong, and I read it again and again and again.

Over the next few hours the phone was red hot as people like me who knew him were ringing each other up in disbelief and I can honestly say that no one believed it, even though it was obviously true. Not only did I know him but he once had a pot of tea in my home and I'd often shared a pint or two with him in the pub. On top of that I'd taken him metal detecting with me and introduced him to other people. But the thing that terrified me the most was the fact that he'd been in a ploughed field, metal detecting with my own daughter. I couldn't believe it!

During the course of the following months and at his trial more details started to emerge and the headlines in the paper then were, 'South Yorkshire man who admitted to being the notorious "shoe rapist" may have many more victims who have yet to come forward.' He admitted to being the serial sex attacker who struck across South Yorkshire in the early to mid-1980s; and stealing stiletto shoes from his victims as trophies of his crime. When police raided his business premises they found a secret cupboard which contained over a 100 shoes, stockings, tights, lingerie and a pile of porn magazines some of which were dedicated to shoe fetishes. Some of the shoes belonged to some of his known victims along with jewellery and detectives could not rule out the possibility that some of the shoes and stockings may have come from other victims who failed to report their sex attacks at the time.

James admitted that he began his sickening, sexual crime spree in 1983 when he struck twice, three times in 1984, and once in 1986 – the same three year period that Sally and I were metal detecting with him. He used to use a mask for disguise, and he'd creep up behind his victims and truss them up with tights or stockings which he had brought with him prior to the rape. Each of the attacks was more brutal than the one before and during the last one he produced a knife to terrify his victim with. Apparently when he was arrested two decades after his reign of terror he said, 'I knew that was coming, I was a bastard twenty years ago.'

In court he was described as a respected business man, a Freemason and was regarded as a pillar of society. A cold case review and an appeal on BBC's Crime Watch programme in 2002 produced no new leads for the police and it was the development of familial DNA techniques which secured his arrest. The crime database yielded forty-three people who had DNA with close links to that obtained from the victims of the Dearne Valley 'shoe rapist'.

Enquiries started and when the police interviewed a woman who had been convicted of drink driving and whose brother matched James's description, they knew that they had their man. This woman was, in fact, James's sister. When James sister (who had no knowledge whatsoever of his wrong doings) told him that the police were on their way and wanted a mouth swab from him, he confessed everything to his father and then tried to hang himself.

The police also discovered a document relating to rape which was called the 'Perfect Victim' and this described to a 'T' details which matched the way that James had carried out his attacks.

In Sheffield Crown Court he admitted to four violent rapes which had taken place between 1983 and 1986 and a further two attempted rapes; and outside the court the police said that he may have attacked many more. The judge condemned him as a coward and he was jailed for at least fifteen years. The judge also said that if James, who'd admitted to the offences, had been found guilty after a trial then he could have expected a fixed term sentence of thirty-five years, adding that few sexual cases were more serious than these and that he had been living a lie since the rapes appeared to have stopped in 1986.

Although I curse modern gadgets and gizmos, the evil crimes committed by James might have gone undetected for ever, without the modern technology and techniques available to the police today.

The very fact that the police's commitment and tenacity in opening a 'cold case' enquiry after twenty years bears witness to the fact that a criminal can never brag that 'he's got away with it' and I take my hat off to the whole team who brought him to justice – well done!

I've always been taught to be cautious but both I and other people who also knew 'the shoe rapist' never suspected a thing, and all agree that out of a line-up of 100 people he would have been the last one to be picked out.

It just goes to show how we can all sometimes get things wrong and misjudge someone. I've been around the block a few times during my life, but the thoughts of me innocently introducing my own daughter to a serial rapist during the time that he was active, still haunts me today. It's my opinion that the old adage 'leopards don't change their spots' is true and I have to ask, 'Why did he suddenly stop?' Somewhere out there, there could be more victims.

Lessons learned!

Health permitting, I'll be telling you some more interesting and funny stories in my next book. I leave the CID and go back into uniform when everything is less serious and we can have some great laughs. See you then; but meanwhile all the very best and thank you for reading this book.